FROM THE OUTHOUSE
to the
WORLD

A GLOBAL TOUR OF THE MIND AND SOUL

JACQUELINE SEGARS BEHRENS

Copyright © 2015 by Jacqueline Segars Behrens

FROM THE OUTHOUSE TO THE WORLD
A Global Tour of the Mind and Soul
by Jacqueline Segars Behrens

Printed in the United States of America

ISBN 9781498423007

All rights reserved solely by the author. The author guarantees all contents are original and do not infringe upon the legal rights of any other person or work. No part of this book may be reproduced in any form without the permission of the author. The views expressed in this book are not necessarily those of the publisher.

Unless otherwise indicated, Scripture quotations are taken from the King James Version (KJV) – public domain

www.xulonpress.com

DEDICATION

I dedicate this book to my mother and father, Ruth and Raymond Segars, for loving me and teaching me Christian values; and to my sister, Patsy, and my brother-in-law, Bill Grisham, who encouraged Mother and Daddy to support my going to college. These were the best gifts they could have given me to create a global tour of my mind and soul.

Mother and Daddy

Also, I dedicate this book to Forrest Lee Behrens, my husband, who has walked this journey with me by giving so unselfishly of himself to support/ participate with me in my career, accepting my demanding travel schedules from home a month at a time, and being with me at so many

Patsy and Bill

international student activities. To this day, all mail, emails, Mother's Day cards, and phone calls from former students always remind me to say, "Hello to Forrest."

Jacque and Forrest

Forrester, you are the love of my life, my rock, and my tranquilizer. You are my best friend! Words are inadequate to express my love and gratitude for giving so much of yourself to me and our international students.

TABLE OF CONTENTS

Foreword by Dr. Larry Keefauver ix
Introduction:From the Outhouse to the World xi

Chapter 1: Childhood Memories (1943-1954).... 13

Chapter 2: Tough Times Don't Last; Tough People Do (1954-1965) 27

Chapter 3: Teaching/Learning Days (1965-1969) .. 40

Chapter 4: "Here Am I, Send Me" (1969-1971) .. 52

Chapter 5: Far Away Places with Strange-Sounding Names (Summer 1971) 74

Chapter 6: Sweet Home Alabama – Transformation Time (1971-1974).... 90

Chapter 7: A New Life in Texas (1975-1978) ... 102

Chapter 8: Voyage of Discovery (1978-1980) ... 116

Chapter 9: Looking Forward, Looking Backward (1981-1993)............ 136

Chapter 10: Climb Every Mountain Until
You Find Your Dream (1994-2003) . . 153

Chapter 11: Life's Roller Coaster (2003-2004) . . . 176

Chapter 12: God Is Not Finished with Me Yet
(2004-2015) 187

Final Word 195

FOREWORD

What a joy and inspiration it has been for me to know Jacquie and to hear all the wonderful ways God has used her to touch people for Christ around the world. No one could have imagined that from her impoverished and humble beginnings that she would have opportunities in life to abound in Christ in every way. She had so few resources in material things, but she had great wealth in being loved in a Christian home and knowing the living God whose resources and grace toward her are unlimited!

As you read this book, I encourage you to have some tissues close by as there will be moments when you will want to cry. Her experiences will bring tears of pain and of joy to you, and you will laugh and rejoice with her as well. Doors around the world for meeting interesting people and sharing Christ with many different people groups have opened in amazing ways for Jacquie. You will be amazed. Yet, there is more in these pages than just one woman's story of journeying through life from an outhouse to the world.

You can find yourself in these pages. You can discover that no matter what you lack in material, intellectual, emotional or spiritual resources, God will be your source if you let Him. You may feel like a no body, but in Christ you are somebody. He has a purpose and a wonderful journey for you as you serve and follow Him. Jacquie experienced lack, suffering and pain, yet she discovered that God was at work in everything in her life for good (Romans 8:28).

I am excited for you as you journey with Jacquie through this book. God will speak to your situation, circumstances, suffering, pain, and problems with hope, healing, and encouragement. Through what Jacquie has learned about God and herself, you will discover truths about God's purpose and resources for your life's journey.

So sit back, take time, and relish this journey. It is like a rich, warm, Thanksgiving meal with family and friends that overflows with godly conversation, amazing stories, and the presence of God. After reading this book, you will feel like you have feasted at the Master's table, and you, too, will experience the goodness and mercies of God for your journey through life.

-Larry Keefauver, M.Div., D.Min., Texas Christian University

Bestselling Author and International Teacher

INTRODUCTION

FROM THE OUTHOUSE TO THE WORLD

And we know that all things work together for good to them that love God, to them who are the called according to his purpose. (Romans 8:28)

Jacquie Segars Behrens

I grew up in a Christian home and learned to trust and have faith in God as I sought to do His will. I really was a very naïve girl who was loved by my family. In high school I had a very low self-esteem. I did not feel like I fit in since I did not have money to spend on events, no fine clothes, no car, and could not even stay after school to socialize because I had responsibilities at home.

Dr. Ken Chaffin of South Main Baptist Church in Houston taught me a whole new way to read and learn from the Bible and how being a Christian was fun. Today, I see so many young people and adults wandering the streets with no focus for life and no plan for a career. In this book I want to show how with God's guidance, I went from an **Outhouse to the World**. Without God, I would have continued in the path of a girl living a life in a little house with cracks in the floor with no resources to experience life.

I survived health issues, received an education that led me to teaching, then on to graduate school, and finally to my goal to work with international students. None of this would have been mine without God's presence and guidance every step of the way.

CHAPTER 1
CHILDHOOD MEMORIES (1943-1954)

No matter where life takes you, don't forget where you came from!

I was born in Decatur General Hospital, Decatur, Alabama to Ruth and Raymond Segars. Both of my parents grew up in farming families in the rural areas of Morgan County. Daddy had a fifth grade education. He had some illness as a child that prevented him from being accepted into active military duty. In 1943, he was diagnosed with disabling Rheumatoid Arthritis (RA). Daddy had the severe crippling kind of RA with bones projecting out at joints. A group of doctors came to the house to take Daddy to Birmingham, Alabama on Saturdays to try to determine what caused this severe RA.

One time, the doctors got him a jug of orange oil from the skin of Florida oranges and had him rub it on his joints. The house smelled like oranges, but this oil did not help the RA. Another time, the doctors had him drink turpentine, but it was of no help. Daddy was one of the first to try the Gold Shot, as it was called, which was the first cortisone they developed. **It worked!** I am sure the doctors got the shot for Daddy, for we could never have afforded the $75 it would have cost in 1950. Daddy was a guinea pig during the initial search for the causes and treatment of RA. We were so happy that someone was trying to make Daddy feel better.

The day after receiving the Gold Shot, Daddy got up early and started a fire in the old coal stove we had in the living room. He was so happy. Mother, my sister Patsy, and I were so giddy from such joy that Daddy could walk and use his hands. He was not in pain; his eyes were not yellow and sad. It was an amazing discovery or so we thought.

Unfortunately, this did not last long. Daddy got sick to his stomach from taking the shots so he had to stop. Our house was filled with sadness as we grieved for our Daddy having to live with so much pain! The doctors did not want to give up so it was back to trial and error. It was back to Daddy sitting in his chair all day until I came home after school to feed him and give him his medicine.

Hospitals seemed to be a big part of our lives. I remember one time Mother was in the hospital for quite a while, and Decatur General let Mother pay $5 a month for years to pay it off. She was so proud when she finally was able to pay her debt. She did not depend on someone else to help her. She taught me to be responsible for my own debt.

> **If there is no struggle, there is no progress. (Frederick Douglass)**

God Has a Purpose

On Sunday mornings, I would hear the pastor say, "God has a purpose." My heartfelt question was, "What purpose is there in suffering and pain?" There was a constant struggle in my heart as to why my Daddy had to suffer so much. Sometimes Mother would have to take Daddy to a chiropractor to manipulate the area around his lungs. He could not breathe without severe, sharp pain. I looked around, and there were mean people who were not suffering.

"My Daddy is a good man, why does he have to suffer?" I would ask.

Mother, Daddy

Mother, Daddy, Patsy, and me

Mother had an eighth grade education. I remember her struggling to work as a waitress for $12 a week, and studying so she could take the GED equivalency test and receive her High School diploma. She did it, too! She began to teach Sunday school. I would read in her notes about God healing the blind men in Matthew 9:27-31. I wondered why my Daddy had not received the healing we were all praying for. In Romans 8:28 I read, "And we know that all things work together for good to them that love God, to them who are called according to his purpose." I wondered what good could come from Daddy's suffering. I had my struggles with all of this, but I also felt the presence of God in my life. Somehow I knew in my heart God must have a reason, even though I did not understand it at the time. I chose to put my trust and faith in Him even though it hurt me to see my Daddy suffer so much.

Humble Beginnings (1943-1954)

My sister, Patsy, was five years older than I. We shared a bedroom as we were growing up, and we learned to share the responsibilities around our home as well. We had a pig, a couple of chickens, and I had five kittens that Mother and Daddy said I could keep as long as I took care of them. Because Mother worked, Patsy would cook supper and I was her helper. We took care of washing and drying the dishes even though I had to stand on a chair to reach the counter top. Wanda, my playmate, and I used Ajax or Comet to make the old aluminum pots and pans shine. Of course, once Patsy and I cooked something in them, they turned dark again. To clean the house, I turned the hose on and rinsed the floors off, and the water, dirt, and dust ran through the cracks between the planks on the floor. Obviously, our home was very cold in the winter because of those very same cracks in the floor.

We always ate a good breakfast of fried eggs and bacon and then ate lunch at school. Supper was usually fried potatoes, pinto beans, and cornbread without meat unless somebody killed a hog, a cow or caught fish, and gave us some. We did not have desserts. On Sunday, Mother put a roast and vegetables in the oven before we left for church. I would think about the delicious meal and could hardly wait to get home. Sometimes, she would make a chocolate or coconut pie for Sunday dessert as a special treat.

Mother worked hard, studied at night school, and sewed all our clothes as well. I remember she used flour sacks to make my dresses when I started first grade. I was so proud of them. She was a very talented seamstress that helped her later in life, too.

Outhouse for 11 years

We even had an outhouse instead of an indoor toilet. In the winter, I waited as long as I could before making that trek to the outhouse. Our visits to the outhouse were short, certainly no reading room like many bathrooms seem to be today, that is unless you liked to look at the Sears' catalogue.

We bathed in a big round aluminum tub. Taking a bath was not a luxury. It just had to be done. In the winter it could be a chilly experience!

> **Mother worked hard, studied at night school, and sewed all our clothes as well.**

Our home at the end of 1402 15th Ave SE, Decatur, Alabama was surrounded by sweet-smelling honeysuckle vines and three pima cotton fields. As a child, I remember pulling a long cotton sack and picking cotton. I think I made fifty cents a day when the opportunity was available. We had no toys; and for Christmas, we got fruit. We did not know any different. Our lives were full. All of the neighborhood children seemed to come to our house to play. All the mothers knew Daddy would be on the front porch keeping an eye on us and watching us play.

Usually, we played rock school, and I was the teacher. Old black, tiny pebble stones and dirt made the road since it was not paved. Big Mulberry trees were in our yard which gave us lots of ideas for creativity. We used the Mulberry leaves as buns and made hamburgers from that old dirt. One time, I made a six-layer black wedding cake using the leaves as dividers between the layers.

We were all happy. We created our own fun. We loved being outside and interacting with the other children in the neighborhood.

One of my favorite things to do as we got older was to ride inside an old car tire down the little hill on the side of our house next to the cotton field. We could go pretty fast. Then one of the Southern Airline planes from Pryor Field would fly overhead, and I would jump out of the tire and follow the airplane until it was out-of-sight. I was so fascinated with airplanes and the people on the plane. Who were they? Where were they going? How much did it cost to fly? I wished I could fly somewhere. During this period, I heard Connie Francis sing, "Faraway places with strange-sounding names." The song played over and over in my head. Someday I wanted to be able to fly somewhere wonderful and see some of those faraway places with strange-sounding names!

Laughter and Fellowship

I remember when Brother Freeman was our pastor, he and some of the church members liked to come to our home after the Sunday evening service. Mother would go into the kitchen and cook up some biscuits and gravy. My Mother made the best biscuits and gravy! This was better than any Champagne dinner with steak and lobster. The laughter was loud and joyous. Everyone had a great time and eagerly anticipated the next visit even though we did not have chairs for them to sit in.

One Sunday evening, some gentlemen of the church came to visit Daddy, supposedly to cheer him up. Instead, Daddy was witty, and they were the ones who enjoyed laughing until tears flooded their eyes. I can still see Daddy wiping his eyes with those bony, deformed fingers. He had laughed so much his eyes were filled with tears. Laughter is truly the best medicine. What a wonderful attitude my Daddy had! He was not going to let these men have a pity party because of his condition. He lifted them up. Often some of them would give a gift to Daddy, especially during hospital times. Friends were wonderful!

Laughter is the best medicine. What a wonderful attitude my Daddy had!

One time, the men came and enjoyed this merriment with Daddy. At the end, they asked Daddy if I could go to Church Camp with the other children. Someone had given the money to send me to Camp as a special gift. Daddy was pleased that someone had invested in his little girl! I have wonderful memories of camping with my church friends.

Maybe it was the times, but my parents did not show much affection to one another in public even though they loved each other very much. They did not show much affection to Patsy and me either, but we knew they loved us just the same.

I remember coming home from Church Camp and sitting on my Daddy's knee as I told him of my adventures. He kissed me telling me how much he had missed me. He had not shown his emotions like that before, and it really warmed me up inside. Among my Mother and Daddy's families, they seemed more reserved with their emotions as well. I remember someone telling about Grandfather not kissing my Grandmother until they got engaged. Times sure have changed!

While I was still in elementary school, Mother got a job at Good Year Mills. We did not have a car so somebody gave my mother a ride to work every day. Mother's job at Good Year was using her hands to direct the threads as they ran through the machine. Because Mother was such a good seamstress, she was valued in her work. I do not remember exactly how many years she worked there, but one day she came home saying that the new Chemstrand plant was coming to Decatur and needed a seamstress to work in its Research Department. Somebody from Chemstrand called Mother's supervisor and asked whom he would recommend for this job. The supervisor recommended Mother. Mother got the job in fabric research at Chemstrand, and it provided her with a salary and insurance. We all were so happy! Good times were ahead for our little family!

It was at this time that Mother and Daddy bought a little car that had two seats in the front for Mother and Daddy and a rumble bucket in the back that Patsy and I could sit in. If it rained, we held an oil table cloth over our heads. I remember when we went to Grandmother's house, we had to stop at the bottom of the moun-tain where spring water trickled by. We would have to get out and put water in the car before we could drive on to Grandmother's house. We were as happy as we could be!

Daddy and I in front of the car with the rumble bucket

Reflection Questions

Think back for a moment to how you were raised.

- *How did the things you saw your parents face as they worked to provide for your needs shape your work and life decisions?*
- *What kind of legacy are you leaving for your children when it comes to dealing with family and life issues?*

Read Romans 8:28.

- *What does this verse mean to you?*
- *Do you know the purpose of adversity in your life?*
- *Do you want to learn how you can resolve your problems?*

My prayer is that as you read my story, you will learn the importance of trusting God every step of the way, in good times and in bad.

Action Steps

Begin your own journey toward trusting God during the good times and bad by reading and meditating on these verses from the Bible. As you read each one, write down what the verse means to you and how it applies to where you are in life right now.

1 Peter 2:4 says I am _____

What does that mean to me and the struggles I am facing today? _____

John 16:33 says in this world I will have _____ , but _____

What does this mean to me and the struggles I am facing today? _____

Romans 8:31 tells me if God _____ who can come _____

What des this mean to me and the struggles I am facing today? _____

1 Corinthians 10:13 promises God will not _____

What does this mean to me and the struggles I am facing today? _____

Romans 9:33 promise that those who _____ God will never _____

What does this mean to me and the struggles I am facing today? _____

CHAPTER 2

TOUGH TIMES DON'T LAST; TOUGH PEOPLE DO (1954-1965)

Tough times don't last; tough people do.
(Robert H. Schuler, Chrystal Cathedral)

Strength to Weather the Storms

I can do all things through Christ who strengthens me. (Philippians 4:13)

Good times were ahead, or so we thought. We were all so excited. Mother wanted to renovate the house and put in a commode and shower. We got a better car with four seats, and Mother had riders who helped with the car payments. She was thrifty and managed our money well.

Mother got quotes on renovating the house, but she had to stop plans for the renovation because I got sick. Mother had been taking me to a doctor because my blood count was low, and I continued to receive pints of blood frequently. A woman's blood count was supposed to be about thirteen. Mine was six even after receiving blood. Sometimes I would be standing on the porch and just fall off, as I blacked out. The year I was in seventh grade, I received twenty-two pints of blood.

Mother took me to the doctors in Birmingham, and they said I did not need surgery. So, Mother hired Mr. Hutchinson to renovate the house. The plan was that Mother and I would stay with close friends, and Patsy and Daddy would stay with relatives while the house was under renovation. The house had just been gutted when Mother received word from my gynecologist, Dr. McCoy Pitt in Decatur that I had to have exploratory surgery immediately.

Strength and growth come only through continuous effort and struggle. (Napoleon Hill)

Tough Times Don't Last; Tough People Do (1954-1965)

I sensed something was not good and though I felt confused, Mother had taught me Isaiah 12:2, "I will trust and not be afraid." I tried to remind Mother to trust, but that day she cried and cried. My Daddy was hurting physically as well as emotionally. Relatives, neighbors, and friends all seemed so upset. My room was filled with flowers before and after surgery. Later, I learned Mother went to our old gutted home by herself at 3:00 a.m. the morning of my surgery and dropped to her knees under the bright moon with tears flooding down her face and prayed to God, "Lord, I give Jacquie to you, to serve you. Please do not take my little girl away."

I was in surgery for some time that morning. When I finally got back to my room, I remember seeing people lining the hall at Decatur General Hospital. Some were crying having heard that I had died during surgery. They had come to give condolences to my family. They were surprised and shocked when Mother asked if they would like to come in to see me. All I remember of that whole time in the hospital was that people visited and flowers showered my room. Later, I learned that my father had been taken to the Bank Street Hospital. My Mother was so strong through it all. It was so hard on Daddy physically, emotionally, and spiritually. He was so sick himself that he could not do anything to help us.

In the midst of all of this, I was told that both of my ovaries were encapsulated by tumors each the size of a grapefruit. They were sucking all of my blood. In 1954 my ovaries were removed, but I was told that the uterus was not. The doctors said they could not keep me alive another thirty minutes to remove the uterus, something about I had taken too much blood that year, and I may be immune to it. Mother sat in my room sobbing after hearing the news that I could not have children. I told her not to worry about it. There would be plenty of children to adopt. Patsy told Mother she would have plenty of children for me, too. Patsy and Bill gave three precious children to our family–William Thomas, Stephen Patrick, and Laurie Ann. I am grateful as well that Laurie and her family – Mark, Randall Kay, Will, Patrick, and Andrew live nearby.

*Randall Kay, Patrick, Mark, Andrew, Will,
Laurie, my niece, and family*

Daddy got out of the Hospital before I did, and finally, our home was completed. We survived that very tumultuous time. My parents' love and faith in God was ever-present in our family. I thank God for giving me such great parents and such a loving sister. We worked together to get through the tough times. It was not easy. In fact, our ordeal was heart wrenching, but God gave us strength and courage to do what we had to do.

If God brings it to you, He will get you through it.

Once things settled down again, our next big acquisition was a ringer-type washing machine. We still had to hang the clothes on the line and even got some of those jean frames to crease the pants. We had a commode, a tub, a washing machine, and a hardwood floor in the living room. Patsy and I continued to do the cooking and washing dishes. Patsy did the ironing. Mother even got some new cookware so I did not have to clean those aluminum pots and pans any more. Instead I had the living room hardwood floor to clean. Wanda and I would make a game of the work. We would put the wax on the floor, and then I would pull Wanda around on a towel over the floor to shine it.

I finished the seventh grade at Walter Jackson even though I had been in the hospital. Most of my classmates had no idea why I was in the hospital. I studied and was active in the Junior and Senior Honor Society, Youth for Christ, the Latin Club, and the Thespian Club. I competed and received parts in two plays. In the junior play, *Seventeenth Summer*, at 4'8" tall. I was the pesky six-year old with French pigtails who frequently interrupted Phyllis and Jack during a kiss.

I worked in the Counselor's office, and she told me about a job at NAPA. This was my senior year, and I needed to make money to go to college. I knew Mother and Daddy could not afford to send me. Ms. Webster advised me to apply for the National Defense Student Loan (NDSL), which I did receive.

Daddy and Mother did not want me to go to college. Daddy wanted me to get a job in Decatur so he could take care of me. Uncles on my Father's side of the family were advising my Father not to let me go to college, warning I would become contaminated if I went off to college. Fortunately, my brother-in-law, Bill Grisham, encouraged my parents to let me go. He was enrolled at Florence State College after completing his service in the Navy and knew the value of an education.

> "Without a humble but reasonable confidence in your own powers you cannot be successful or happy."
> (Norman Vincent Peale)

College Days

John Kennedy said that one should think of education as the means of developing one's greatest abilities because each person has a private hope, a private dream, and when it is fulfilled, it can be translated into benefit for everyone and greater strength for one's nation.

After graduation from Decatur High School, I worked at NAPA all summer. In the fall of 1961, my parents drove me to Florence State College (FSC) to Willingham Hall. The room I lived in then was so small in comparison to residence halls today. There was a bunk bed on one wall and some drawers for my clothes. There was no desk. I had to use the shower down the hall. If a man came into the hall, the girls had to shout, "Man on the hall." I received $369 dollars each semester which covered my tuition, fees, books, room, and board. I worked in

Willingham for spending money. If I did well on a test, I would walk to downtown Florence to a drug store on the corner of Seminary and Mobile to treat myself to a banana split for fifty cents.

I had a desire to know about people in faraway places with strange-sounding names. I thought I would learn about that in geography. What a mistake! Geography was about plants and animals in different climatic environments. To make matters worse, this was my first class Monday morning at 8:00. During the very first class Mr. Jonas told the students to read the first chapter which I did. During the next class, Mr. Jonas called on me first. I was the most petite, shy and scared person in the class.

"Miss Segars, how many degrees are there in a circle?"

I answered, "360."

He stopped in his tracks and stared at me, "Are you sure?"

Shaking like a leaf, I said, "Yes, Sir."

He wheeled around on his heels, went to sit on the edge of his desk as he smoked his cigar.

What could I change it to? He would grill me on that. It was 360 degrees.

Then he looked over his glasses at me and asked, "Are you absolutely sure? You still have time to change your mind."

I was silent.

Then he asked, "Are you going to change your mind?"

I answered, "No, Sir."

One could hear a pin drop; it was so deathly silent. There was a long, deadly pause.

He glared at me over his glasses as he smoked his cigar and said, "You are correct!"

I knew I was, and I never liked him after that. I studied and studied for his classes and made an "F" on every test. He did not test on what we were reading. He used trick questions. Almost all of us made "F's." Every morning before I went to his class, I was sick at my stomach and repeated Philippians 4:13, "I can do all things through Christ who strengthens me." I made it through the first semester, including Mr. Jonas' class. When I received my grades for the semester, I made a "B" in his class.

When I went to Collier Library to register for the spring semester, the first teacher was Mr. Jonas who said, "Well hello, Ms. Segars. You did very well in my Geography 101 class; I want you to take Geography 201."

I wanted to register for Psychology to learn more about people, but he erased Psychology and penciled in Geography 201. I completed registration and promptly walked over to the Business Office and paid my money to change courses. I was not going to take him again.

Unfortunately, psychology was not much better. This instructor was a monotone, boring person and gave "True or False" questions that I could justify either way. I made the grade, but I did not learn much in geography or this psychology course. Later, I took psychology under another professor and made an "A." Some people are just not good teachers. They are not good communicators and do not care about their students. I certainly did not want to be like either of these teachers.

One spring while I was studying at FSC, I went to Huntsville to take a test at the old barracks on Jordan Lane. I passed and was offered a job in Technical Publications at NASA. One of my jobs was to type the biography of Werner Von Braun, the director of the Space Center. One fact that I remember is that he failed algebra seven times. Finally he said to himself, "If I want to send man to the moon, I have to pass algebra." He made an "A." That fact stuck with me.

Do not ever let anyone tell you that you cannot do something! Do not let anyone belittle your capabilities! Remember, with God, all things are possible.

Tough Times Don't Last; Tough People Do (1954-1965)

While I was studying at FSC, my Mother was rushed to Decatur General for lung surgery. While in surgery, she got a staph infection and ended up in the hospital for a year. This was a difficult time for Daddy. It was like it was the last straw. He broke down in tears, one of the few times I ever saw him sob. During this time I decided to stay in school, study, and work in Willingham Hall during the week. Then I went home Friday to work at Sears as a floater Friday evening, Saturday, and Sunday.

One department I really did not want to be in was tile and carpet. I did not know how to calculate how much tile or carpet one needed until someone taught me a formula to use. Then I sold more tiles and carpet than anyone and never had a complaint. Thus, for the year Mother was in the hospital, I was assigned to tile and carpet. When I was not working at Sears, I was at home cooking up enough food for Daddy to eat during the week. I felt guilty that he had to stay by himself during the week, but I knew I had to get my education.

Obviously, my social life was nil, but I wanted an education. In spite of Geography, Psychology, and Ms. Kitty Jones, my English instructor who said I would never make it teaching in high school since I was 4' 8" and that I should plan on teaching in elementary school, I made the Dean's list. I graduated in June of 1965 from

Florence State College with a double major in Biology and English. Mother and Daddy came to my graduation in the Amphitheater at FSC on a beautiful spring day.

When we got home, Daddy was so proud of me and said, "Girl, you have an education; nobody can take it from you."

Reflection Questions

1. What crisis are you facing today? Do you have faith in God to see you through?
2. What can you learn from this crisis? Sometimes God must make us uncomfortable in order for us to make a change.
3. What is your goal/purpose in your life? Do you have direction or are you just drifting?
4. Has anyone ever told you that you could not do something? How did you react?
5. What are the obstacles preventing you from reaching your goal?
6. What are your priorities?
7. Is God a partner in your decisions? He may have a better plan than you do.

Action Steps

Continue your own journey toward trusting God during the good times and bad by reading and meditating on these verses from the Bible. As you read each one, write down what the verse means to you and how it applies to where you are in life right now.

Isaiah 12:2 exhorts me to say, _____

Philippians 4:13 says I can _____

Proverbs 4:7 tells me how important it is to _____
_____

Proverbs 23:23 tells me to _____

James 1:5 promises that if I lack _____ all I have to do is _____

And _____

How do these scriptures apply to my goals and my priorities for my life? _____

CHAPTER 3
TEACHING/LEARNING DAYS (1965-1969)

Teach me and I forget; Involve me and I learn. (Benjamin Franklin)

After graduation from Florence State College, I got my first teaching job just outside of Atlanta, Georgia. Barbara Williams, who graduated from FSC a year before I did, invited me to live with her, Billie Ann, and Polly in an apartment in Decatur, Georgia. I taught at Lithonia High School. Science teachers were in greater demand than English teachers; therefore, with a double major in biology and English, I taught biology.

My first teaching year was difficult. I had several lesson plans to prepare daily. I diligently studied how to best teach each course and developed a plan for each day. I had to do this or the students would know I was not prepared, and I would not have their attention. Norman Vincent Peale said, "Enthusiasm makes the difference." I over prepared my lessons so that I would not be embarrassed in class. I taught Biology as if it was the most important subject. Ever Garrison says, "A teacher is a compass that activates the magnets of curiosity, knowledge, and wisdom in the pupils." That was my goal.

My salary was $4,000 a year. I worked harder that year than I did in some future jobs. It was an old school and rather run-down, but in general it was a good year. I had to be careful with money, for I had to pay the first-year installment on my loan. My English teacher at FSC had said I would not make it teaching in high school, and here I was teaching seniors and enjoying it. Even though all of my students were taller than I, if some of them talked I just stopped teaching and stared at the talking student or students. Then the whole class would stare at whoever was talking.

However, during one lab we were dissecting cats to observe the different body parts. I had to stop class several times to ask Jeff not to talk. Finally, I asked Jeff to come back after school. He begged me not to make him come after school because he was the Basketball Manager and had to be at practice.

Jeff came after school and I asked Jeff to clean the lab tables. He was so angry that he poured too much powdered cleanser on the black lab tables. He tried to wipe the tables off, but bubbles kept bubbling up. I started helping Jeff, but it got to 5:00 p.m. and we were still cleaning. About this time, the Coach and team came to my room looking for Jeff. They saw the problem, and the Coach directed the team to start wiping off the lab tables.

I do not know how Calhoun Community College in Decatur, Alabama got my name, but the English Department needed an English teacher in the fall 1966. Someone from the Department called me resulting in my packing up my belongings and returning to Decatur prior to the next semester. Mother and Daddy wanted me to live with them. I agreed with the condition that I would pay monthly rent. I wanted my independence. I had reservations about moving home because I thought they would try to treat me as their little girl again. College had not contaminated me, but I had learned to think for myself. However, living with Mother and Daddy was a wonderful, meaningful experience. I enjoyed being with them.

There were about six single teachers that I befriended while teaching English Composition at Calhoun. If someone caught some fish that week, Mother would fry catfish and hushpuppies on Friday night. Mother's hushpuppies were the best. She put onions in them which made the hushpuppies delicious and tender. Linda, Ann, Shirley, Phil, Mike, and Richard loved to come over for home-cooked food. Somehow we managed to sit around a small metal table in the kitchen that was supposed to accommodate four. Friday nights were cozy for sure and filled with laughter.

It certainly changed Mother and Daddy's lives. These friends would often stop by and visit with Daddy, who loved the company especially while Mother was at work. Even after I completed my one-year contract at Calhoun and moved to Birmingham to teach, they often came one by one to visit Mother and Daddy for years afterwards until they moved on in life. I appreciated their friendship and respect for my parents. These additional personalities certainly energized my parents' lives for years and made my year at home enjoyable.

I remember that there were mostly young men in one of my English composition courses at Calhoun. They really did not have good English skills. They did not know what a complete sentence was, and they could not grasp what the subject and verb were. I even diagrammed sentences trying to help them visualize a sentence. One of the assignments was to write a short paper with a themed topic.

After grading the papers with a red pen and returning them to the students, one of the young men said, "You are just sending me to Vietnam. I am going to write you every day and tell you how bad it is there."

Another young man responded, "She will grade it in red and send it right back to you, and it will be bleeding, too."

That stung my heart, but I could not pass them if they could not communicate orally and in writing. How did they pass English in high school if they could not write a sentence? I wanted to help the students, but I wanted to be honest with their future employers. I tried to improve my teaching techniques to help these students learn to write a complete sentence. Back then they did not have computers to help them with spelling. I completed my one-year contract with Calhoun and paid my second installment on my loan. I often wonder how and where those men are today.

In the summer of 1967, I joined a National Education Association tour of about twelve countries in Europe: England, Portugal, Spain, France, Monte Carlo, Italy, The Vatican, Liechtenstein, Austria, Switzerland, Germany, and a few others. I finally got to visit some of those far-away places with strange-sounding names. I vividly remember being in Spain on July 4. The trip was great, but I was deeply moved not being in the United States on Independence Day with family. In fact, this emotion surprised me. Someone put a tiny American flag at the front of the bus. I wonder how many of the others on the bus felt the same as I? It seemed that everyone was quietly thinking of home in the United States. I stopped to thank God truly for my country. This was my first short journey away from home. I cannot imagine the passion our soldiers feel while away and when they step back on American soil.

My next teaching assignment was at E. B. Erwin High School in Birmingham, Alabama. I taught Senior English and English Honor Students. The School was new and the Principal was most supportive. The students were lively and overall happy. I enjoyed my classes. These students energized me. They were so curious, interested, and willing to learn. It was like I could not give them enough. There were lively discussions in the classes.

An assignment that came with my job as Senior English teacher was to direct the Spring Senior Play. I made a mistake in allowing a meticulous Fleur de Lis design to be on the stage wall. It took the students forever to paint the three walls. Rehearsals started and day after day, the lead actor, Bruce, did not know his lines. Of course, the other actors could not get their lines in sequence with Bruce either. The other students and I became very frustrated. What should I do? Take Bruce out? Would someone else learn the lines in time for the play? At the dress rehearsal, Bruce still did not know his lines. The students and I became most frustrated. This rehearsal was useless. I closed down the stage, turned off all the lights, and told the students to go home. They begged me not to stop the rehearsal. I went home with a heavy heart laden with shame, uselessness, embarrassment, and a sense of failure. I was in tears. We had worked so hard on it. I had let down the Principal, all of the other actors and actresses in the play, all of the E.B. Erwin students, and the Center Point community. I had no worth. I was so alone. I did not share this with anyone.

I was nervous, anxious, and paranoid the next day. I did not tell the Principal. Would I be fired after the play failed? All I could think of was that Kitty Jones said I would not make it in high school. Now I wondered if I would make it anywhere? I really do not remember anything about that day. Evening came. The stage lights came on. The parents and teachers, other students, and friends from the community were pouring in and chattering with glee. I could not hold my head up; I was so embarrassed.

As the stage curtain opened and the play began, all the players including Bruce were saying their lines perfectly. What happened? How can this be? Intermission came. People in the audience were happily chatting and enjoying themselves. I ran across the stage hugging and kissing them all. They were doing a wonderful job. Mr. Cummings, a favorite teacher of the students, came on stage and congratulated the students. Everybody was on a high. Even though Mr. Cummings had been a little reserved to me, I even hugged and kissed him. The second half was as perfect as the first; they even included the tips I had offered during practice. When the play was over, the audience stood and applauded over and over.

> **Ralph Waldo Emerson said it best,
> "The secret in education lies in
> respecting students."**

I was overwhelmed with awe! What happened? How did they do it? We had never had a good rehearsal. Later, I learned that the characters in the play kept Bruce up all night drilling him on his lines and their lines. Good for them! It worked. Never underestimate the power of the students motivated to achieve. I slept well that night and I bet they did, too. There was excitement the next day, and I joined in all of it. Students are fun! They just wrapped themselves around my heart in so many ways. I wonder what Bruce is doing today. I bet he is successful in spite of himself. What are the other characters doing? As for you Ms. Kitty, "Yes, I can."

Albert Einstein said, "Life is like riding a bicycle. To keep your balance, you must keep moving."

Life demands struggles. "No Struggles; No Progress." Students kept me humble in my efforts to make a difference in their lives. In addition to teaching them from my lesson plans, I discovered students often wanted and needed counseling. High school students especially have a way of "saddling up" next to a teacher to subtly ask for counseling. I realized their questions were so important to them that they became brave enough to ask for help. They often melted my heart, but I also learned it was important for me to care and be realistic at the same time. Students needed to learn through their struggles. It was a tough balance. I just wanted to hug them and make everything okay, but I needed to help them learn how to identify for themselves how their struggles could be managed. This is a growth spurt for them.

> **Margaret Mead taught, "Children must be taught how to think, not what to think."**

After getting through this school year, I regained confidence again to make my life the best that I could. Abraham Lincoln said, "To predict your future is to create it." My yearning to see more faraway places was still an ear worm in my head. I completed an application to teach overseas. One more year down and another payment on my loan.

> **Nahi Lam says, "Every day, we are given the chance to make our life better; what we did yesterday has already made our life better today and tomorrow has already benefited from what we are going to get out of today."**

My teaching days prepared me to be a teacher of English as a Second Language in Japan. My life experiences prepared me to leave my comfort zone and go to a strange place to live and to survive. I was ready! I had faith God's presence would be with me all the way.

Reflection Questions

1. God was preparing me to gain confidence in my abilities and empowering me to teach overseas. In what areas of your life have you asked God for experience and confidence to face a difficult challenge? In what areas of your life do you need God to prepare you? Have you discussed it with Him?
2. The more you pray to God in all honesty and with the right motive, the stronger the relationship you have with God. Then He will identify opportunities for your life. Do you feel and know God's presence as you reach for your dream?

Action Steps

Continue your own journey toward developing a closer relationship with God. Read, meditate on, and discuss verses from the Bible with God as you spend time with Him every day. Just like any other relationship, the only way to really know someone is to spend quality time with them. As you develop a closer relationship with your Heavenly Father, journal what He reveals to you each day.

Psalm 145:18 _____

Teaching/Learning Days (1965-1969)

Psalm 145:19 _____

Psalm 145:20 _____

CHAPTER 4:
"HERE AM I, SEND ME" (JAPAN 1969-1971)

Creating a new me! The best way to predict your future is to create a new you.
(Abe Lincoln)

The thought of being a missionary had floated in the back of my mind since elementary school when I read Isaiah 6:8, "And I heard the voice of the Lord saying, whom shall I send and who will go for us. Then said I, Here Am I, send me." John 4:35 also rang in my ears, "Look up your eyes and look on the fields; for they are white and ready to harvest."

Many denominations had a journeyman program whereby people younger than twenty-seven could assist missionaries for two years. I applied to the journeyman

"Here Am I, Send Me" (Japan 1969-1971)

program and listed the countries of interest to me. I was interested in Jordan because of my desire to know more about biblical lands. My last choice was Japan, but God said it was the best place for me. After a thorough application process, I was selected to go to Fukuoka, Japan which is on the Southernmost island Kyushu of Japan. It is a port city in the area that was supposed to be bombed instead of Nagasaki, but it was clouded over so the planes flew south and dropped the bomb on Nagasaki instead.

I started orientation for training to go to Japan as soon as I completed my teaching assignment at E. B. Erwin. I listened and listened to Japanese tapes. Learning and speaking Japanese was very difficult as I found I could not get my tongue twisted in the right position to make some of the Japanese sounds. God made me a poor language student so that I would have some sensitivity for my students.

Packing for Japan was a challenge. Cassette tapes were popular at the time. Therefore, I recorded a lot of music and selected some books I wanted to read, all because I thought I would have some alone time in my little *tatami* (straw floor) apartment. I packed both summer and winter clothes. I carried all I would need for two years in nine suitcases. I cannot describe the flood of emotions that I experienced all summer as I prayed, studied, said farewells, and did my best to convince my parents I would be okay. Daddy wanted his little girl to stay home so he could take care of her. I even had a steady boyfriend who carried all nine suitcases to the airplane in Pryor Field for me.

There was a tsunami of emotions the day of departure. I was sad to be leaving Mother and Daddy, but anxious to complete my commitment to teach students and see the world to learn about other people and their cultures. I was really concerned about leaving Daddy. Would he live until I returned? I believed I was following God's will and had to put my trust in Him. I continually repeated, "I can do all things through Christ who strengthens me" (Philippians 4:13). This was a time of great faith, and I felt very close to God. I was leaving my family and all that I knew to live in a totally different place. My anxiety level was very high.

The Japanese students must have known the teacher was coming. They were at the front door of the house in which I would be living. As I unlocked the house, they welcomed me asking, "How does it feel to be from the richest country in the world?" I do not remember anything else. I must have slept for days.

When I awoke I began to look around. I thought I would be in a small apartment with tatami floors. This

"Here Am I, Send Me" (Japan 1969-1971)

house had five bedrooms, a nice library, a dining room, a big refrigerator, stove, washing machine, dryer, and a big living room with a fireplace. This was more than I had ever had in the States. I would share this house with Mary Lynn Anderson from Lubbock, Texas. Mary Lynn was tall, intelligent, thoughtful, loving, and reserved. She was assigned to teach English as a Second Language (ESL) at Seinan Gakuin University, and I was assigned to teach ESL at Seinan Gakuin High School.

Seinan Gakuin

Both the University and the High School were just across the street from where we lived. Our house was one block from the Pacific Ocean where there was a marker stating Genghis Khan came on shore there. There were many missionaries in Fukuoka, and most of them lived across the campus from us. The missionaries gave us a warm welcome reception, and the students were awesome.

In addition to our assigned classes, we taught Bible classes Sunday morning and evening. Sunday mornings, I taught a Bible Class in English at Kobayashi Mission and in the evening at Seinan Baptist Church. Students from the University, High School, and many who came to my professional classes at the American Consulate, the YMCA, and even classes I taught at home came to my Bible classes. God had given me an opportunity to share God's love in my actions and caring spirit.

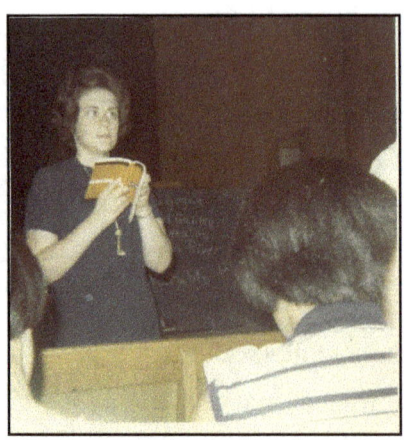

Jacquie teaching a class

At different times, students would come to me and ask, "Why are you a Christian?" I explained as simply as I could. Whereas in the States I would have answered with a Bible verse; there I had to translate them. The verses had so much more meaning to me when I translated them into words that the students could understand. In addition to my school and church classes, I had classes in the evening at home, the American Consulate, and the YMCA. Mary Lynn and I did not see each other much because her students carried her in one direction and my students in another. We were teaching day and night and felt like we were on vacation.

We learned to shop for fresh vegetables and flowers from Nishi-jin outdoor market. We survived on cooking American food or she prepared Ceviche, a raw Peruvian food. She had lived in Peru for a short time. We canned cucumber pickles that looked and tasted like apple rings, delicious, and eventually even tried to cook some Japanese food.

Skiing on Mt. Daisen, called Little Mt. Fuji

Mary Lynn and I had been in Fukuoka about four months. The University students invited us to go snow skiing to Mt. Daisen on the western side of Japan. We rode on the slow train with fifty students overnight arriving at 8:00 the next morning. The Japanese students had been noisy all night just like American students so I wanted to rest for a while. No rest, no sleep, and a cold breakfast of rice, raw egg and soy sauce, and Green Tea were waiting for us, and then off to the slopes! Two older Japanese men were our instructors. They spoke no English nor understood it. We all gathered outside under a tree to put our skis on. I had never seen a snow ski and certainly did not know how to put one on. It took me awhile. When I finally looked up, the whole class including Mary Lynn was down by another tree on the slope waiting for me. I was so embarrassed.

I started skiing, but ended up flying off in the opposite direction. I decided to enjoy the moment. I started shouting, "Gomen Kudasai" which meant excuse me so they would get out of my way. I did not know how to get out of theirs. I could not believe I was skiing. Finally, I saw a tree that would not get out of my way so I sat down and skied right into the tree with a kiss. "Wow! This was fun!" I thought as two Japanese male students skied up beside me.

"Segars Sensei, you were supposed to ski to the group," they explained.

I had no idea how I was going to get back up the slope so I could join the rest of my group. The students demonstrated how I was to walk with my skis sideways one step at a time back up the hill. It took me an hour to get back to the group. I was exhausted. Everyone had learned how to stop, turn left, and turn right. The Japanese instructors explained, and then it was my time to demonstrate how to make these three moves. I did it. I was so proud of me. I was the Sensei which is a title of honor given to a teacher. I had to do it, I could not fail.

"Here Am I, Send Me" (Japan 1969-1971)

By this time, I was thinking, where is the hot chocolate and fireplace? The Japanese did not take a break until lunch. We had thirty minutes to eat our curry beef, steamed rice and Green Tea, and we were to get back on the slopes. It was snowing ice and was miserable outside after lunch. This was not snow. The sun was not shining. About 6:00 p.m. we called it a day and were finally taken to our room. I got my futon and put it on my plank attached to the wall and laid down in the fetal position to try to get warm.

Mitsuishi San said, "Come on, let's go take a bath."

In my mind, I saw images of a Western hot tub that would get me warm. Mitsuishi San took us to the public bath. I unrobed myself and jumped in. Then I looked back to see that other women were sitting by the pool with a little bucket of water washing off. Where did they get their buckets? I had contaminated the water by not washing off. Maybe I should have looked before I jumped in the warm pool. Well, I got warm, rushed out of the pool, wrapped a towel around me, and went to my room. The rest of the evening was fine. We were served Shabu Shabu which is thin slices of lamb that is swished back and forth in a tasty broth with vegetables served over steamed white rice. Then I sat by the fireplace drinking Green Tea instead of hot chocolate. I slept soundly all night even though I was sleeping on a plank with a thin futon.

The next day we were taught to jump up with our skis when we got to the edge of a cliff and turn downward. If we did not do it correctly, we landed in the top of a tree after falling off the cliff. I observed, and finally it was my turn. I landed in the tree top. So much for the Sensei Model! The following day, we were taken to the top of Mt. Daisen and could see the Sea of Japan in the far distance. I was sick to my stomach looking down. I could just imagine myself skiing right into the Sea and drowning. I was at the back of the line with wet noodles for legs. I fell many times as I continued to entertain the students and the Japanese instructors who stayed behind me. I was humbled, but at least they would not leave me behind.

We finally arrived at the bottom of the mountain, got on the train to head back to Fukuoka, but I do not remember the trip back. I was exhausted. I must have slept for a week during our New Year's break until classes started again.

Adventures in Japan

Mary Lynn and I had been downtown exploring all the department stores when we decided to eat at a restaurant nearby. We were trying to read the menu when the waiter asked if we would like a hamburger. We did not think we could get hamburgers in Japan. We waited and waited, then he came out with chopsticks and a plate with a couple of asparagus. We exchanged glances as we waited. The milk shake came out, but it was a raw egg in milk that was shaken with no ice cream. We waited some more. Finally, the two-inch thick hamburger arrived between pieces of white bread. There was no lettuce, tomato, mayonnaise, or ketchup. We ate a few bites of dried beef and politely left. We just were not hungry anymore.

There were two boys that were Mary Lynn's University students who wanted to learn English so they could visit the Grand Ole Opry. They could sing country western songs just as well as the Opry singers. We enjoyed listening to them. One time they took us to a fish farm to let us fish. Of course, we caught fish. They cooked the fish, steamed rice, and Green Tea, plus they serenaded us with memorable country songs. The boys did make it to the Grand Ole Opry in Nashville. I often wonder what they are doing now?

Whenever there was a holiday, the professional students about my age wanted me to go with the group to a shrine or temple. A shrine was a happy place for weddings and celebrations while a temple was usually for sad occasions like death. The Japanese would tie a prayer onto the limbs of the trees. As a group, the students came to a consensus as to where our next trips would be such as Nagasaki, Hagi or some other pottery places. I think we went to every pottery kiln in Kyushu and some on Honshu Island. One of my favorites was Koishiwara pottery in Kyushu. A petite older, bent-over Japanese woman with a scarf over her head invited me to go into a kiln with her. She picked up an elegant round black vase with a streak of white lightening that had a crack in the side. She was so sad. I told her I liked and wanted it. She was overjoyed that somebody liked her work even though it was cracked. She thought it was worthless, and I thought it was beautiful. I have it today displaying an artificial flower arrangement.

When I lived near Atlanta, Georgia, I tried to wear contact lens. The doctor must have tried twelve different pairs for my eyes, including a very tiny one that just covered my cornea. My eyes were in pain, swollen and puffed up so I quit trying. However, while I was in Fukuoka, I thought the Japanese make such great cameras, maybe I could get some contacts here. One of the missionaries made an appointment and went with me to see the Ophthalmologist.

I sat down with great confidence and looked for the big "E." When the doctor asked me what I saw, I said it looked like a spider. He laughed. He asked me through the missionary translator to describe where the openings on the spider were. I did my best. When he put contact lens in my eyes, I could see. I wore them home and never had a problem for two years. As I was preparing to return to the States, I went back to the Ophthalmologist and got another pair for $72, much less expensive than what I would have been charged in Atlanta.

One night a week, I taught ESL at the YMCA to professional students who were about my age. Some students came to me after class to tell me that Dr. Hashiyama, a cardiologist, wanted to drive me home. I usually rode the street car at night. It was a fun ride. The streetcar was filled with chubby Japanese men with red cheeks who had been drinking at the saki bars. We always looked forward to seeing one another, bowing and laughing, but we never talked. But on this night, Dr. Hashiyama wanted to drive me home. I would get to ride in a car for a change. However, he was nervous. Dr. Hashiyama bumped off other drivers' fenders and kept going. When we got to my house, I got out and thanked him vowing never to ride with a student practicing his English ever again.

One evening I invited the students to my home so they could see an American home. They were to bring Japanese food, and I would prepare some American food. It was a potluck! They prepared fish foods, and I prepared green beans, Jell-O which they did not like, and cornbread which was a good old Southern food. I was in the kitchen getting our food ready to serve. The Japanese students kept coming in and opening the refrigerator door. The refrigerators in their homes, if they had one, were about the size of a small refrigerator used in a dorm room. In the midst of all this, Dr. Hashiyama came in to tell me I was to sit next to him. It was after the fact that I learned that Japanese initially date in groups. As I reflect on some other group events, I may have had other dates of which I was unaware.

Another one of my professional student classes wanted to take a trip to Hagi. I wanted to get some Hagi Yaki. This was the pottery that previously only the Emperor could give as gifts. The students all had cars so we drove some distance, checked into a traditional Japanese Inn with the tatami floors, got into our yukatas – a casual summer kimono made of cotton. We enjoyed some Green tea together sitting on the tatami floor with a very low table on which to place our tea cups. It was a fun evening. The ladies and I were in one tatami room with individual futons and the guys in another.

I made a few mistakes on this trip, too. I misread the sign on the bathroom door in the hallway and thought I was going into the Women's side, but found myself side-by-side with a man. The next morning, I decided to go

"Here Am I, Send Me" (Japan 1969-1971)

to the Public Bath before anyone else got up. I was alone and enjoying the warm pool. Toward the end of my enjoyment, I looked outside just as the sun was coming up. There were fishermen with their boats parked next to the window looking in on me. In a dash, I was out of the pool, robed myself, and away to my room.

Some of my male students from the University Sail Club told me they had a new boat that they wanted to christen *Jackie,* and asked if I would go with them to an island off of Fukuoka to christen it. The wind was blowing so we got to the island in a short time. We christened the boat and headed back as I had a class to teach at 9:00. However, the wind was blowing against us. Fortunately, with their skills, we did get back just in time for me to teach my class.

One day I was on the streetcar going to downtown Fukuoka to shop. The people on the streetcar were mostly older Japanese and seemed rather tense as they stared at me. I knew what they were thinking.

Finally, one little boy broke the tense silence to ask, "Mama, Gaigen deska?" During the war, Gaigen meant "Red Devil."

I smiled at the little boy and his Mother and said, "Hai! Watashi-wa Gaigen; Watashi-wa Sensei at Seinan Gakuin. Yes, I am an American teacher at Seinan Gakuin."

I could sense the relief of the passengers in the streetcar. They smiled, bowed, and expressed gratitude for my living and teaching in their city. Mary Lynn and I became well-known in Fukuoka, especially at the bank, post office, and at the market where we bought fresh broccoli, zucchini, other vegetables, chicken, and fresh flowers for my flower arrangement class. Whenever I wanted to eat out, I went to a little Tempura Bar with eight bar stools and ordered a tempura plate that included lightly battered shrimp, fish, sweet potato, chrysanthemum leaf, and zucchini with some hot green tea. Delicious! Now I miss tempera as much as I missed hamburgers in Japan.

One Saturday I rushed to the one grocery store at Nichijen-machi to get some powdered sugar. I needed to make a cake for an event that evening. The store did not open until 10:00, but the doors were open so I rushed in. I found my powdered sugar and a few other items, but the manager told me I could not shop because the store was not open. I pretended I did not understand so he took my little basket from me and put it on the floor behind the cash register. I stood by the cash register until 10:00 sharp, checked out, and rushed home to ice my cake. I left the house in time to get to my next class.

That night a group of students were at the house, and we had a delightful meal. Then I proudly served my cake.

"Here Am I, Send Me" (Japan 1969-1971)

The icing was so pretty until we took a bite. It was deathly bitter; we all spit it out. The bag I bought was clear, and the powder inside looked like confectioners' sugar. The students told me I had bought Monosodium Glutamate instead! They got great pleasure out of my mistakes.

One rare Saturday night when Mary Lynn and I were home together listening to the Radio station from Hakata Air Force Base, the music was interrupted when Paul Harvey came on to announce that there had been a severe tornado in Lubbock, Texas, and told the name of the building that was twisted in downtown. Mary Lynn's father worked in that building. She immediately tried to call home to see if her family was okay. After a time of waiting with high anxiety, she learned that her father and family were safe.

My dear friend, Judith Melicks, was working with the Red Cross and was stationed at Camp Zama near Tokyo to help with the soldiers who were injured during the Vietnam War. She came to Fukuoka to visit me and offered to take me to the Commissary at Hakata Air Force Base which was about an hour train ride from Fukuoka. This was a real treat. I lost myself in the Commissary as I walked down the aisles filled with Del Monte canned beans, corn, tomatoes, and so many more vegetables. I went to the dairy section, and there was cottage cheese which I had not had since I left the States. Then I floated through the meat counter which had ham, hotdogs, and buns that were not available to us at Nishijen-machi market. I loaded up with canned vegetables, cottage cheese, pineapples, hotdogs, buns, and ham. When we checked out, I had four heavy bags of groceries for the two of us to carry on the train back to Fukuoka. The total cost was $13 which I planned to pay. Judith paid saying it was worth $13 dollars just to watch me shop. She said it was more fun than any movie. It was truly an appreciative treat to me!

Lessons I Learned in Japan

My Ikebana Sensei was an older Japanese woman who spoke no English. I observed how she arranged the flowers and tried to imitate what she did. She would say, "Subarashii (wonderful), Sensei" and carefully rearrange the flowers. I never got it exactly right. Tanaka Sensei, the Principal of Seinan Gakuin High School and my calligraphy teacher, would teach me how to meditate and then draw the Japanese character. He, too, would say, "Subarashii Sensei," "Wonderful, Sensei" and then took my hand and redrew the character. I have hanging in our home a scroll with "I am the Light of the World by Jacquie Segars - watashi wa yo no hikari desu." I finally did it.

Jacquie standing next to her 125 year old hibachi and her calligraphy

My Ikebana (flower arrangement) Sensei told me that our Ikebana group was going to march in one of the Festivals and wanted me to march with them. I put on my Yukata and Geta – wooden shoes and marched for an hour or two. My students were on the sidewalk and yelled my name. All of the residents of Fukuoka knew about this American Sensei in Fukuoka, and they were pointing at this Gaigen and laughing. I returned a smile and waved at all of them in spite of the big blisters forming between my toes from those wooden shoes. I had fun!

During a school holiday in 1970, I decided to take bananas to some missionaries in Seoul, Korea. I had an eight hour, tatami floor with futons boat ride at night, then rode a Greyhound bus from Pusan to Seoul, Korea. After a long ride, I finally arrived to meet some of the Korean missionaries who were so grateful for the bananas for their children. The poverty in Seoul made me sad as I watched small children trying to pick up trash to earn money to have rice that night.

I also wanted to go to Panmunjeon, the tense military demarcation area between South and North Korea that was still separated by barbed-wire fence. One of the male missionaries took me in an open jeep which was a requirement so that we could see what was happening above us. There were fox holes along the way. One of my former doctoral students at TTU became the Mayor of the West city that borders Panmunjeon. When I visited him in 2002, he gave me a plaque with some of the barbed wire fence I saw in the 70's. It is hanging in my home. I have visited there several times since then. Korea is now a very modern, developed country.

In 1970, the Baptist World Alliance was held in Tokyo. Mary Lynn and I were asked to work the conference. We did a lot of typing, took guest speakers from one place to another, and got to attend some of the sessions.

This was an exciting experience, and we got to meet and visit with many leaders around the world.

Mother's Visit

Mother saved her money to visit me in Japan. I was in Tokyo at the time and met her at the Narita Airport and saw her as she came through Customs and Immigration. We went to Kyoto and on to Osaka for the Expo "70" -The World's Fair in Osaka, Japan. Mother and I spent the whole day viewing the new architectural designs. We were ready to leave and went to the train station. There was a train there, and it was ready to leave for Kyoto. I ran and jumped on just as the doors closed on my arm. Mother was still on the outside. If the train had actually left, I could not have gotten off for an hour, and then it would have been another hour back to Osaka. Since, I had my arm in the door, I knew it would open. Finally, the doors re-opened and Mother jumped in. Whew, a tense moment.

There were a few sad times while we were in Japan as well. Mary Lynn's boyfriend who was in the Military came to see her; but when he got back to the States he was killed in a helicopter crash. My boyfriend quit writing after a year or so.

Twenty years after my return to America, some of my former Japanese students invited Forrest and me to come for a twenty-year reunion. What a gift to be able to see what my students had become! They were grown adults with wives and precious children. Now, I could see the boys as men and giggly girls as ladies and still *speaking English with a Southern accent*.

Reflection Questions

1. Have you ever thought God was calling you to do something? How did you respond?
2. Have you ever been still enough to hear/listen to God? To know His presence?
3. How do you prepare yourself spiritually to commune with God and know of the opportunities He offers? As a Christian read the Bible, pray, listen to God, and feel the presence of God.

Action Steps

Begin your own journey toward understanding the calling of God on your life. Read and meditate on these verses from the Bible. As you read each one, write down what the verse means to you and how it applies to where

"Here Am I, Send Me" (Japan 1969-1971)

you are in life right now as you seek God's purpose and calling on your life.

Romans 8:30 _____

2 Peter 1:3 _____

Psalm 46:10_____

CHAPTER 5
FARAWAY PLACES WITH STRANGE-SOUNDING NAMES (SUMMER 1971)

"The world is a book and those who do not travel read only one page." (St. Augustine)

It was June, 1971 and two years had passed so quickly. The movers came to pack and ship our goods. I had 900 pounds of pottery. I used the pottery as dishes so I did not have to pay customs on it when I entered the States. Coming home, I had a small suitcase that held only thirty-three pounds. I was the faculty adviser to the students in the English Club; and all those high school boys came to my home the last day of my teaching and sang, "Leaving on a Jet Plane" and "Auld Lang Syne." Those boys still have a special place in my heart. I hugged each one of them, even though they were reserved. They had been so faithful and loyal to every event. I miss them.

Another tsunami of tears at the airport with students who brought flowers and cards from all of my classes, especially my professional students who became my best friends and taught me so much. All the other missionaries who had supported me, my Japanese language, Ikebana, and Calligraphy teachers were all there as well. The airport was full. Words are inadequate to express those last moments at the airport and my love for them. Tears flowed between Fukuoka and Taipei. I was torn between two cultures. I was now a multicultural person.

As I reflect on Japan, the development of and appreciation for my new self-concept was the best learning experience for me. I did not have to do what other people expected me to do. I could be me. At the end of two years, I liked me as I was. I developed confidence because I had to depend on God working in and through me. I came home a mature adult. *My past and my education had been my tutors to prepare me for this adventure.* I had a fantastic two years of experience even though I worked hard day and night. God gave me a unique opportunity to demonstrate His love and to make a difference in other people's lives. He gave me the courage to step out in faith.

> **"Without a humble but reasonable confidence in your own powers you cannot be successful or happy"**
> **(Norman Vincent Peale).**

I decided to take a month and travel by myself around the world via Taiwan, Hong Kong, Macau, Thailand, India, Turkey, Israel, Russia, Denmark, and then to New York. I wanted to include Egypt, but I had an Israeli visa in my passport; therefore, I was denied a visa to visit Egypt.

Taiwan, Hong Kong, Macau, and Thailand

I knew a journeyman in Hong Kong and Taiwan so that was helpful. We saw all the significant places in Taipei such as Dr. Sun Yat-sen Memorial Hall, Chiang Kai-Shek Memorial Hall, and then I flew to Hong Kong. Hong Kong is rather small so we saw all the significant places and shopping centers in about two days. I remember we went to the top of a mountain and looked over into China to see the communal villages and the gray armed boats policing the Pearl River that flowed through Macau. I felt uncomfortable in this spot. We visited Macau that was occupied by the Portuguese and was rather undeveloped. It was a significant historical place.

I went back to Macau in 2011. It is now a modern, commercial city filled with casinos.

From Hong Kong, I flew to Thailand. Ms. Graves, my missionary neighbor, made arrangements for me to meet one of her friends in Bangkok who met me at the airport and took me to see the majestic temples in Bangkok. He gave me a piece of ivory that had twelve balls cut within one piece of ivory. Amazing handwork! We attended a dance of many beautiful Thai ladies dressed in gorgeous silk material. Their hand motions were fascinating to me. Bangkok is magical, decorated with majestic golden pavilions, the floating market, and decorative palaces.

Adventures in India

From Bangkok, I flew to Delhi, India. Up to this point, I knew someone in each country who would assist me if needed. I did not know anyone in India, plus the airplane would not fly into the Delhi Airport until after dark. I was a little unsettled to think I had to get to my hotel in the dark. I had heard the taxi drivers would try to charge too much. My plan was to talk to somebody on the airplane and get advice as to cost, protocol, etc. There was only one empty seat on the whole plan, and it was by me. I sat in my seat pondering what to do when a Texas-Ranger looking guy came back to sit in the seat next to me.

This man was the President of Toledo Steel in Ohio. His daughter went to Harvard Medical School with an Indian medical doctor whom he was going to visit in Delhi. I asked him about how much to pay the taxi drivers.

He said, "Oh, don't worry, my Indian friend is coming to pick me up at the airport, and we will take you to your hotel."

We talked the whole trip. He came to India often and was bringing some gifts to his Indian friend. Finally, we landed in pitch black. There were no lights anywhere as we see in the States. I went through Customs with no problem.

As I waited for my Ohio friend who was further back having to open all his bags, taxi drivers were reaching for my little suitcase. I finally had to put it between my legs and faked sitting on top to stop them. They still surrounded me. Finally, my friend came out of Customs and met his friends and brought them over to meet me. We were stacked in layers in his little car and drove away from the airport. The headlights on this car were about the size of a small flashlight as we drove through mass darkness until we arrived at the Janpath Hotel. I said my goodbyes and expressed my gratitude for their assistance. I fell

Faraway Places with Strange-Sounding Names (Summer 1971)

in bed and set my little alarm clock so I could get up early in the morning to go see the Taj Mahal in Agra.

I was up at 5:30 a.m. I took a bath, dressed, and went to the restaurant to have a cup of coffee and a piece of toast. As I was about to sit down, I heard a man's voice say in English, "Well, you don't have to sit by yourself." I looked around and there was an American-looking man sitting at a table having his coffee. I picked up my toast and coffee and went to sit with him. He was about fiftyish and asked what I was going to do. I told him I was going to take an air-conditioned bus for $60 to Agra to see the Taj Mahal. He said he was taking an air-conditioned train for $30 to the Taj Mahal. We finished our coffee and hired a taxi to the train station.

The sides of the road were covered with homeless people. Walking through the train station was a sight I cannot get out of my mind. There were hungry people lying on the floor of the train station. We had to step over bodies to get to the ticket line. Finally, we were at the back of the line waiting. The man left me. As I neared the front of the line, he returned with a young Indian boy who was maybe twenty. He told me this young man would take us to the Taj Mahal in his car for $15 each. He was dressed very neatly and spoke excellent English. Off we went to this young man's car. But when we got to the car, there was an older Indian man sitting in the passenger's seat.

I remember thinking, "Jacquie, you are getting into this car in India with three men you do not know. Mother would have a fit if she knew I was doing this."

At 7:00 in the morning we were on our way to Agra. The young man explained everything to us as we passed different villages. The American man and I were in the back seat.

Later, the driver turned to us and said, "Now if the Police stops me, tell him that I am taking you and your wife to the Taj Mahal as a favor to my brother in California from where you live."

"What?" I whispered, "I am not your wife."

He said, "Shut up!"

There was absolute silence for a while, and then we saw an elephant in the middle of the road. The driver asked if I would like to ride the elephant. When I said yes, he stopped the car. The elephant was so big that my head was under its stomach. I rode the elephant down the middle of the highway.

About 10:00 a.m. we were out in the middle of nowhere when the driver pulled off to the side of the road. There were a lot of older Indian men wearing their white robes on the side of the road, chatting, laughing, and smoking their pipes. We were told to get out of the car for a break. I was the only woman. An older, very wrinkled man with a bag walked over to me. A python raised its head out of the bag and continued to raise its body upwards as the old man played his recorder. I ran away from him. Finally, we got back in the car and drove on down roads of nothingness.

Finally the stunning architectural beauty of white marble came into view. The Taj Mahal is one of the most famous buildings in the world. The driver gave us a personal tour of the Taj Mahal and explained that it was built by a Muslim ruler of India in the 1600s in memory of his wife. Unfortunately, thieves had carved the jewel stones out of the white marble. The driver then took us to some sites to buy a souvenir. I bought a tall brass tea pot. It really was a good day even though I had gut-wrenching anxiety at times when I did not know what was happening.

On the way back to Delhi, the driver asked if we wanted to see a small Indian village. The village had very few people that I could see. The family we visited lived in a cave, but I saw a radio at the back of their cave room. Other people lived under the tree. There was a bed under the tree that looked like the biblical pictures, "Take up your bed and walk." There were four legs with a canvas or cloth stretched out to each leg. It was light and easy to carry from one tree to another.

Whenever I go anywhere, I want to see more than the touristic spots. I want to know how the people live. I was very happy that we stopped to visit. As we drove back to Delhi, daylight turned to massive darkness. I do not know if I have ever experienced a total blackout like I did in India. The little flashlights on the car helped the driver to stay on the road. There were no streetlights; there was total darkness.

As we neared Delhi, the American man asked if I would like to go to dinner with him that evening. He knew a restaurant that was on the ninth floor of a hotel that served delicious food. I wanted to know who this man was. We had been surrounded by people all day and could not talk openly.

"Yes, I would love to."

We went back to our rooms in Janpath and showered. It had been 116 degrees outside, and we were sandy and filthy. I had to use another one of my three dresses; therefore, I had to wash two of my dresses by hand, the one I had when I flew to Delhi, and the one I had worn today. I needed one for tomorrow.

Dinner was delightful and when I asked who he was, he calmly smiled and said he was a missionary from

California to India. Since it is illegal for a missionary to get a visa, he was there on a tourist visa. God sent the Toledo Steel President and this missionary to be my guardian angels in India. The missionary told me all about his family, and I told him about my family. He explained a lot about India.

I told him I wanted to see the Red Fort and Million Dollar Street. He said he would go with me that I should not go by myself. We visited the Red Fort first and then went to Million Dollar Street which was covered by village vendors. I did not buy one item from them though they all came to grab my arm to come shop with them. At one time, I was surrounded by vendors and could not move until the missionary came over and took my hand to lead me out of that area. That night I packed my two little dresses and prepared to depart for Israel, thankful for God's protection over me in India.

Israel: The Land of Jesus

There was a missionary meeting me in Tel Aviv and taking me to Jerusalem, Bethlehem, Jericho, and the Dead Sea. Israel may be a tiny country, but there is so much history there. We went to Jericho and then the Dead Sea. Jerusalem, one of the oldest cities in the world, is between the Dead Sea and the Mediterranean Sea. A highlight of Jerusalem was the Via Dolorosa, where Jesus carried the cross. We saw the fourteen Stations of the Cross, ending at the Church of the Holy Sepulcher–a pilgrimage for millions of Christians. We saw Mount Zion, Mount of Olives, and then we went to Bethlehem to see the Church of the Nativity. A young man met us at the Church and invited us to his home. His sister served us bread, cool cucumbers, tomatoes, and cheese. Delicious!

We also went to the Sea of Galilee, a land-locked sea where Jesus ministered and gave the Sermon on the Mount, walked on water, calmed the storm, and fed 5,000 people. Then we went on to Nazareth, home to the carpenter Jesus. What a blessed journey to walk where Jesus walked!

Cool as a Cucumber in Turkey

Located between Asia and Europe and near the Mediterranean Sea sits Istanbul with all its majestic historical places. The Blue Mosque is so very dominant in Istanbul sitting on a hill showcasing its awesome example of Istanbul's Imperial Ottoman Mosque with cascading domes and its tall, slender minarets. The Topkapi Palace, home to sultans, and Hagia Sophia, with Byzantine architectural beauty, have their own interesting history.

Of interest was the Bosphorus which is a narrow strip that connects the Black Sea to the Mediterranean. Geological evidences support that sunken cities may be along the Turkish coastline, and maybe Noah's Ark is there beneath the Black Sea as well. In ancient times the Black Sea was landlocked. An earthquake destroyed the barrier and connected the Black Sea and the Mediterranean when the water flooded into the Mediterranean and split the City of Istanbul into two divisions–part in Asia and part in Europe. There are other studies that give reasons to believe Noah's Ark rests on Mount Ararat in East Turkey.

As a traveler, I knew not to eat food from street vendors because of the cleanliness. I did not want to get sick with a bacterial infection. I broke this rule. I was so hot; my dress was wet. I learned the meaning of *Cool as a Cucumber*. They were so good and fortunately, I did not get sick.

Russia

I flew on to Moscow on an Aeroflot plane in which the carpet on the floor was coming off, and I could see the metal floor. Certainly did not make me feel safe.

Fortunately, my seatmates were a sweet, older couple from Illinois that were going to Russia to see family members they had not seen in twenty years. They told me about their family's struggles in Russia.

In making preparations for my trip to Russia, I used a travel agent in Tokyo. He advised me that Russia would not tell me in advance which hotel I would be staying at in Moscow. He said some man would meet me in Customs and give me my hotel reservation slip. Sure enough, a nice young man met me in Customs and told me which hotel I was assigned to. As I was getting in the taxi, the young man asked if he could ride with me because he needed to go to this hotel.

The clerk would not check me in until this same young man told her to. I picked up my suitcase and started up the stairs to check in with the Floor Key Clerk. She would not give me a key until this man told her to. I went to my room which was rather nice and spacious. I do believe my room was bugged since apparently there was some question as to why a single woman with twenty visas in her passport was in Russia, June 1971. I went outside and walked around the Kremlin and the Red Square to see Saint Basil's Cathedral and Lenin's Tomb.

The Russians had given me two breakfast coupons and told me where to eat so the next morning I got in line at that restaurant. The clerk at the cash register would not take my coupon. I was holding up the line behind me until a nice Russian man came to my rescue, yelled at the woman, and she eventually took my breakfast coupon and served me a hard-boiled egg, kraut, and bread. Even though I did not request it, the Russians assigned me to a Tour of Moscow. The tour guide did speak English and took me to the Moscow River, the Church of the Savior, Moscow State University, and Kremlin. I tried to talk to the tour guide, but she stayed with her script.

The tour guide announced that if anyone was in a hotel by Red Square and had to catch a flight tomorrow, they should leave for the airport in the morning as the Square would be closed for a ceremony for the four Cosmonauts that died in their shuttle landing. I was disappointed because I had purposely scheduled to be in Moscow on Sunday so I could go to Moscow Baptist Church.

I was hungry and did not know where to eat. I walked the streets until I found a place that looked like a restaurant, but nobody spoke English so I just pointed to some line on the menu. Fortunately, it was beef and rice. There was a Gum Department Store inside Red Square I went to look for a souvenir. Then I went to St. Basil's Cathedral and then to the Opera House before I went back to my hotel and prepared to leave Moscow early in the morning even though my flight from Moscow to Copenhagen was not until late that night.

Denmark

The next morning I went back to the same place for breakfast, but the clerk would not take my coupon. I did not get to eat that day. After arriving in Copenhagen, I checked into my hotel and went to find food. I found a restaurant serving a smorgasbord and ate to my heart's content. There was a place called Tripoli in Denmark that was an enjoyable garden with water fountains. This was just what I needed after the stress of being in Russia. Later, I explored Copenhagen and enjoyed being in such a clean and friendly nation. I saw the Denmark boy and the Mermaid before it was time to pack up and go to Sweet Home Alabama!

Reflection Questions

1. God was my guardian angel during this trip. I had faith, but sometimes I questioned my decision to travel by myself. God took care of me. Have you ever taken on a project that was much bigger than

you and knew God was your guardian angel? List the ones you remember.
2. At what time in your life have you experienced your greatest faith in God? What incident or event led to this time?

Action Steps

Read and meditate on these verses on faith. Look up faith in your concordance and continue to study it on your own.

Write the definition of faith using Hebrews 11:1 _____
_____

Hebrews 11:6 says it is impossible to _____
God without _____

What did Jesus say about faith in Matthew 17:20-21?
_____

CHAPTER 6
SWEET HOME ALABAMA – TRANSFORMATION TIME (1971-1974)

> "Each of us has a fire in our hearts for something. It's our goal in life to find it and keep it lit." (Mary Lou Retton)

My last night in Copenhagen, I was so excited that I would be home soon. I did not sleep well. Mother, Daddy, Patsy, Bill, and others were at the airport to welcome me home. I thanked God every day that Daddy was still alive. It was so good to embrace Mother and Daddy again. We went to get my little suitcase, but it was not there. That little suitcase was with me around the world, but it could not find its way from New York to Decatur.

Sweet Home Alabama – Transformation Time (1971-1974)

Family Patsy, Daddy, Mother, and Jacquie at the airport

When I got up the next morning, I did not have anything to wear. I had left all my clothes in Japan. Word got out and people immediately planned a Layette for me which was like a baby shower. Ladies brought many pant suits with tunic tops. I had never seen this fashion. There were no dresses! I wondered how long these pant suits would be in style?

The neighbors planned a Welcome Home event in our backyard. They had it all decorated so pretty with yellow ribbon, balloons, and six-foot tables covered with food galore. I was excited to see everyone, but by the third day I was ready to go back to Japan. I was more *Junko*, my Japanese name, than I was Jacquie because I had been immersed totally in a Japanese village for two years. I tried to talk to people about the love of the Japanese people and some of my experiences, but their eyes glazed over. Even

Mother and Daddy did not want to hear about it. They wanted to tell me about an aunt or uncle so and so who was sick. Everybody was talking *small talk*. I wanted to talk about the world and the wonderful people I had met.

I did not sleep the last night in Copenhagen nor the first few nights at home. I felt like I was going crazy, crying, and not knowing what to do with myself. Finally, Mother and Daddy took me to the Emergency Room. The doctor gave me a shot to help me sleep. I experienced how horrible Reverse Culture Shock was in comparison to Culture Shock.

Later when I was at TTU, I drafted and did some research for my dissertation on Reentry: Reverse Cultural Shock for Malaysian students. I was detached from everyone. I could not relate to my family, relatives, friends, and neighbors even though they were all so kind. We did not have anything in common. I felt so alone.

All of the returning journeymen were to go to Glorieta, New Mexico for a debriefing. I even felt alone with the other journeymen. I do not know what song was being sung because I was talking to God. I told Him I did want to be here. I wanted to be a missionary in Japan.

I fussed at God saying, "How easy is it to recruit missionaries? I am ready to go to Japan! And You will not take me?"

Sweet Home Alabama – Transformation Time (1971-1974)

I was in tears. My heart was crying. This was absolutely the worst struggle to date that I ever had with God, and I did not know what to do.

While the other journeymen were standing and singing, I felt this soft, misty cloud seemingly drop from my head to my toes, and the message was, "You will not go back to Japan."

I have never had this experience before nor since, but I was having a big problem with God. I could not understand why. What was I to do in the States? I was hurt because He was so firm in His response. During my depression, one of the Japanese girls whom I assisted mailed a beautiful water-colored kimono with a peacock made of gold threads to me. I sat down and sobbed, for I knew I would not be going back. A few years later, Baptist missionaries were removed from Japan. Again, God knew what He was doing. He knew why I should not return to Japan.

Jacquie wearing kimono

This was July and school started in August. I learned of a Senior English teaching position at Tanner High School. I applied and was hired. After school started, there was a meeting of the English teachers to announce there was a need for a sixth grade English class. I volunteered to teach it as well. This school year was the worst year of my life. I did not want to be there, but I did not know where I was supposed to be. I was pretty depressed and hurting. I felt like I had nobody to whom I could talk who would understand.

I knew God had spoken rather firmly. I was to stay in the States. I knew I did not want to continue to teach. I wanted to work with international students. Even with this state of mind, I tried to be the best teacher I could. It was not the students' fault I was unhappy. I tried to be an American again and learn to do *small talk*. That was the boring part.

While teaching my sixth grade English class, one little guy was as cute as he could be. Then one morning he announced that his mother was having another baby, and they would get $13 more dollars a month. A month later this same student announced that his father had quit work. He had worked for 125 days and now he could be off 125 days. These students taught me about the American Welfare system in the 70's. They already knew how to take advantage of taxpayers. This bothered me. This was so different from my Mother's attitude of being so proud for staying off Welfare. She worked so hard for so little

Sweet Home Alabama – Transformation Time (1971-1974)

as did many hard working taxpayers. Their taxes were now going to lazy people who boasted about abusing the system. I saw this same attitude among some of the seniors in my classes.

I knew for sure I wanted to work with international students. I sat down at an old Smith Corona typewriter with a faded ribbon and typed fifty letters to universities in Alabama, Tennessee, Georgia, Louisiana, Florida, and two in Texas. When I was at FSC, I heard someone say something about Texas Christian University (TCU) winning a football game and that name stuck with me.

I wrote, "I have just returned from a two-year ESL teaching assignment at Seinan Gakuin, the American Consulate, and YMCA in Fukuoka, Japan. I would like to do my graduate work in Student Personnel in Higher Education with a concentration on international education. I need a full scholarship and will establish an international office for international students at your university."

I received a phone call from the Vice President at Texas Christian University, who asked if I could meet him in Birmingham as he was on his way to a conference in Atlanta. I met him at the airport and we talked. He hired me as a Graduate Assistant with a full scholarship. My task was to establish an international office at TCU in Fort Worth. Perfect! Exactly what I requested! God had been at work for me all of this time. I was to start the summer of 1972. Now I had something to eagerly anticipate. I was no longer floating without direction. I had a reason to push forward and grow.

> *And be not conformed to this world: but be ye transformed by the renewing of your mind, that ye may prove what is that good, and acceptable, and perfect, will of God.*
> (Romans 12:2)

It is through suffering and crisis that opportunities materialize. God gives us perseverance to strengthen our endurance which builds character and gives us hope to seek His will for our lives. Faith leads us to the next opportunity that God makes available to us. When there is a crisis in our lives, we have to make some changes that often lead to an opportunity that is much better than what we can imagine.

God was working within me, opening my mind through prayer and communicating with His spirit within me. He was trying to transform my thinking from being a missionary and reshaping me to be an international student counselor.

When I got over my pity party, I was able to listen to God. He says in Psalms 32:8, "I will instruct thee and teach thee in the way which thou shalt go." He gave me a new dream and prepared me to work at a university counseling international students. I believe God was working on my behalf the whole time. I just did not have the patience to wait. He knew that TCU needed an international student adviser to establish its international office. There were only 142 students, but there was to be an increased international student enrollment. TCU now has a large population of international students and an active education abroad program.

God was on the lookout for me, but I had to promote my skills and needs in finding a university to give me the scholarship. Faith is dynamic; it requires action. I could not just sit back and wait for God to hand a scholarship to me. I had to contact universities, too. I had to be proactive in finding a way that was congruent with His will. Individuals must be in God's will, and He will walk with us in our adventures, careers, achievements, and failures.

My energy level was filled with enthusiasm again. I had a purpose to help students. I had worth again. I could dream again and hope to reach my goal of counseling international students. When God rejected me as a missionary to Japan, I did not know what to do with my life. It was through this crisis that God gave me the opportunity to go to graduate school to advance my education further and to prepare me to be an international student counselor at TCU working with international students.

That summer, I loaded my car from the floor board to the top with sheets, towels, pots, pans, and dishes. Leaving Mother and Daddy this time was as bad as leaving them for Japan. Daddy had recognized that his little girl had grown up, but he still wanted to protect me. I believed this was God's plan for my life.

I had never been to Texas before, and I really did not know anything about TCU. I lived in a little efficiency apartment paying $65 a month. There was a petition to the bathroom, and a curtain to separate the bedroom from the kitchen and living space. However, graduate school was great! The faculty members took a special interest in my endeavors and were very supportive.

At the end of my first year, Daddy was in the hospital dying with cancer, emphysema, and RA. For three or four weekends, I would leave TCU Friday at 4:00 in the morning and arrive in Mother and Daddy's driveway at 5:15 in the afternoon. I would stay at Decatur General with Daddy while I was there. Sunday I drove back to Fort Worth and studied until late on Sunday night for classes the next day.

The last weekend I was home, Daddy died. I could not cry. He was not in pain any more after thirty years of debilitating pain. The doctors never found any treatment to relieve his pain, but now he was at peace. When I returned to TCU, the staff in the Dean of Students' office presented me with a monetary gift because they knew I had to spend extra money for gas to cover all the trips I made back and forth to Decatur.

I completed my graduate work, and the Dean of Students offered me a job that she had created just for me as Assistant to the Dean of Students. I was to continue to develop and manage the international office. That program was growing, plus she gave me extra assignments to work with American students. Life was good. I was making some money now, and I had a steady boyfriend who was an aerodynamics engineer. We dated while I was in Graduate School at TCU, but he was a dedicated Catholic and I was a dedicated Baptist. I just did not think that would work. Also, John wanted children and I could not have children. I told him we could adopt children, but he wanted to have his own. We were unequally yoked in a couple of ways.

> *Those who wait on the Lord shall renew their strength; they shall mount up with wings like eagles, they shall run and not*

be weary, they shall walk and not faint.
(Isaiah 40:31)

Reflection Questions

1. Have you ever been in the depths of loneliness like I described? Did you try to find your way by yourself? What happened?
2. Have you considered going to God and asking for guidance? God wants us to call on Him for help.
3. What is your dream? Goal? Purpose?

I believe that a girl should not do what she thinks she should do or what others think she should do, but should find out through experience what she wants to do in conjunction with what God has purposed for her to do.

Action Steps

Begin your own journey toward discovering God's purpose for your life. Remember, if you do not know where you are going, you will not know when you get there.

Read James 2:14-18.

Write this passage out in your own words.

How does this passage apply to you personally where you are in your life right now?

Have you confirmed that your dream, goal, and purpose are in alignment with God's will for your life?

If you have, what is God telling you is your next step toward fulfilling it?

CHAPTER 7
A NEW LIFE IN TEXAS (1975-1978)

The great mistake you can make in life is to be continually fearing you will make one. Anonymous

University of Houston

One day while working in my office at TCU, I received a call from a counselor at the University of Houston (UH) International Office saying, "Jacquie, we have a vacancy for an international student counselor's position. Do you know of anyone that might be interested? How about you? We would like for you to apply for the job."

I did apply and was hired as an international student counselor. Dr. Jack Burke, the Director of International

Students and Services and a devout Christian, gave me responsibilities which included working with embassies in Washington D. C. to recruit their government-sponsored students to UH. I was the government-sponsored student counselor.

A group of students were evacuated from the American University in Beirut, Lebanon during the civil war there. They came to UH without transcripts. The faculty advisers placed them in classes as best as possible until their transcripts eventually came. I am still in contact with some of these students from Bahrain, Libya, Algeria, Venezuela, Saudi Arabia, Fulbright scholars and have visited them whenever I was in their countries.

One day, I received a call from the Dean of the Arts and Sciences who asked me to meet with a student whose girlfriend left him for another student. He planned to kill her, her new boyfriend, and himself. He had a weapon and a plan. I counseled with him from 10:00 a.m. in the morning until 4:00 p.m. Then I called the Student Health Center and asked the nurse if she could give him a shot or medicine to keep him calm that night. I did not know while I was counseling this student, but the police were in the office next to mine listening to what was being said.

Forrest, my new friend, was coming over for the first time for dinner and to install my washer and dryer. I tried to cook dinner for him as well as monitor the student until he made it through this crisis. What an emotionally charged day! Fortunately, three lives were saved!

Dr. Burke assigned me to work with the community host families and friends program. His wife and I were to match international students to host families in Houston so that they would have an opportunity to know more about the American family life. This was a wonderful program for international students.

Mrs. Burke felt so strongly about the program that she voluntarily worked in the office to match international students with families to whom she communicated on frequent basis. Many of the families included their international students in family cookouts, little league ballgames, holidays, birthdays, and many of the students went to church with them. If they had questions about the church service, the host family was there to answer the questions.

However, there was one family that we had to remove as a host family. They would go to the airport and meet students on Saturday night which was wonderful. Then after taking them to church the next morning, the family would ask them if they would like to know more about Jesus. Asian students are taught to respect authority or older people so of course they would say, "yes." This family had one student on his knees that afternoon, and later he almost committed suicide thinking he was a traitor to the religion of his family. That family did not receive any more students. As a journeyman, I visited numerous shrines and temples, not because I wanted to convert to Buddhism, but to learn more about the culture.

To have international students in the host family home was educational for their young children as well as the visiting student. Many times the children invited the international students to their classrooms to meet their friends. These students would write home and talk about their host family and what all they did together. Sometimes the host family also wrote to the parents of the students.

A love network was traveling throughout the world between American and international students and parents. This was such a meaningful and far-reaching program for both the students and the families.

Time to Buy a Home

I was tired of paying rent. It was time for me to buy a home. It was one of the original homes built in the fifties when the NASA space program started to grow in the area. I had a home, but not much furniture. I bought a telephone spool and put a sheet over it as a tablecloth.

I bought just a bed frame and mattress. My furniture was very sparse since I had just gotten out of Grad School.

While I was in Houston, I attended South Main Baptist Church. I loved Dr. Ken Chaffin. He did not scream and holler. He was more of a teacher. For example, I have always been sensitive to criticism. I was serious-minded and shy. Dr. Chaffin helped me to understand that constructive criticism was a good opportunity to improve myself. It was at South Main Baptist Church that I met my future husband, although I did not know it at the time. I met Forrest in March 1977 in our Sunday school class and had just started dating him in the summer.

In August, I received a phone call from Dr. Robert Ewalt, the Vice President of Student Affairs at Texas Tech University (TTU), informing me of a position that was available as Director of the International Office. This Office had been under the Dean of Students, but now would be a separate office as of August. He invited me to apply. I replied "No thank you." While at TCU, I said I would never live West of Fort Worth because that is the beginning of the desert."

He thanked me and hung up, and I did not think any more about it. Two weeks later, he called me again. He stated that he had closed the position, reopened it, and would like for me to apply. This time I did, visited TTU, and was hired.

I returned to Houston to tell Forrest I would be moving to Lubbock. He encouraged me to go. He did say he wanted to ask me a question, but did not think I was ready for it. I did not ask what the question was because if it was what I thought it was, I was not ready for it. Within two weeks of our dating, Forrest had told his secretary that he had met the woman he was going to marry.

UH offered me more money to stay, but I had committed to TTU. I thought I would go to Texas Tech, stay two years, and then relocate somewhere else as had been my pattern. But I really did want to settle down somewhere, just not West of Fort Worth. Those two years turned into twenty-seven years. I read in a Business Week magazine that one needed to change jobs every five years to be continually motivated to do one's best. While at TTU, I changed jobs every five years. I developed the international student services including the study abroad programs for American students, the international faculty and scholars program, the international institutional advancement program, and recruitment of international students to TTU.

Forrest moved me to Lubbock. It took us about fifteen hours or more to drive the U-Haul Truck pulling my car.

I lived in one of the girl's residence halls at TTU while I was looking for a house to buy.

A year later, Forrest asked me to marry him. He was very patient with me, for I was afraid to marry since I had met so many who had married, divorced, and were so unhappy. When I asked my *What If* questions, he said, "Let's go see a marriage counselor." I responded that it would cost $70 an hour, and he would want to see us for three sessions. Forrest replied that was the best investment we could make for a successful marriage. How could I argue with that way of thinking?

I flew to Houston and we started our session at 7:00 a.m. one Saturday morning and finished at 10:00. I watched this counselor operate and knew exactly what he was doing. I was a counselor. Why could I not see this between Forrest and me? He asked Forrest how his Mother and Father interacted with each other. He then asked me how my Mother and Father communicated with each other. He explained that even though Forrest and I had come from very different backgrounds, we could be as one in our future relationship. It was at that moment that I really was ready to commit to Forrest.

That weekend, He gave me a one carat marquis that was beautiful. I put it on and it fit perfectly. I was engaged.

A New Life in Texas (1975-1978)

I could not believe it. I felt so comfortable about it. This was Memorial Day Weekend, 1978.

We were ready to get married. School started in August. Since I had not been at TTU for even a year, we decided we would just invite our Mothers to come join us in the Chapel at First United Methodist Church across the street from TTU for our wedding. We called our parents and told them. Mother had married Ernest Chenault after Daddy's death. He reminded me so much of Daddy. Forrest's Daddy had died of a heart attack before he was fifty, and his mother had also remarried.

Our engagement

Somehow the international students heard that I was getting married. They wanted to come to an American wedding. The international women and wives of students came to my office one day and said they wanted to give us a reception after the wedding. The host family ladies helped the international wives. They did it all. I was so busy, I was not involved in this part. I had to contact the church to see if we could reserve the sanctuary. Fortunately, it was available.

A week before the wedding, I realized I had not selected ushers. I had not sent out invitations; therefore, I did not know who was coming. I contacted all of the presidents of the international student associations and asked them to be our ushers. There were the presidents of the Indian Student Association, the African Student Association, Arab Student Association, Chinese Student Association, Korean Student Association, Latin American Student Association, and others.

The wedding was scheduled for Saturday, July 22, 1978 at 3:00. On Thursday evening, we were at the church teaching the presidents of the nationality associations how to seat people, how to light the candles, etc. It was funny to see Forrest's mother when Mohammed Omar took her arm to seat her. She had never seen an Arab before. We had our dress rehearsal dinner at the Great Wall Mongolian BBQ owned by good friends, Harry and Jean Chung.

The day of the wedding, I received a call from Mohammed Shayib to say he could not be an usher because his wife Zhara was having a baby. Walid Shayib was born on our wedding day. Mohammad Omar stood in for Mohammed Shayib.

I doubt that any wedding was as unique as ours. The sanctuary was filled with international students in their beautiful, colorful national dresses, TTU faculty, host families, and some of my international education friends from the University of Texas system, friends from South Main Baptist Church in Houston, and of course, our family members from Alabama and Chicago. We were so surprised. They came from everywhere.

The reception was more than I could have ever imagined. There were Chinese spring rolls, Indian samosas–triangular pastry stuffed with potato, meat, or peas with onions. There were Arabic grape leaves, pita bread with hummus, the Bride and Bachelor's cakes, and so much more. The Chinese had decorated with the beautiful reds and golds for prosperity.

Our wedding picture

The Indians of West Texas had a musical group to play lovely music during the reception, including some East Indian love songs. Beautiful! I could not plan a better reception.

Forrest and I wanted to go to the Grand Canyon for our honeymoon, but the week of the wedding I told Forrest I was tired and suggested maybe we could just go to Carlsbad Cavern for a short honeymoon and maybe go to the Grand Canyon later. We were no sooner out of Lubbock when I fell asleep. I was exhausted from pulling this wedding together that was so much bigger than I ever anticipated.

> **"The supreme happiness of life is the conviction of being loved for yourself, more correctly speaking, loved in spite of yourself." (Victor Hugo)**

In reflecting on my exhaustion, it was not just due to planning a wedding. The Texas Rangers came into my office at 3:00 the week before the wedding to question me about the Iranian students at TTU, and the arrival of the Shah's son, Reza Pahlavi. He was there to take pilot's training. They were concerned about his protection. If any of the TTU Iranian students wanted to play soccer with the Shah's son, I had to seek the approval from the Iranian government.

It had been announced in the newspaper that 1,800 Iranian students from California, Oklahoma, and Chicago were coming to Lubbock to protest against the Shah. Friday, July 21, 1978, the day of my rehearsal party, I was downtown with the Iranian students who were protesting against the Shah and for the Khomeini. What Americans did not know was whether the students were pro-Shah or pro-Khomeini. I was told if a picture was taken of a student marching in protest of the Shah, then his/her family was treated well. That put so much pressure on the students to protect their families.

At the same time, the US Immigration and Naturalization Services (INS) audited our immigration files. We had an accurate record of exactly seventy-one Iranian students at TTU. INS used TTU Immigration component as a model to other universities in the region. The TTU Iranian students frequently marched on campus, but in actuality only two of the seventy-one were really pro-Khomeini.

In 1979 when the Shah was overthrown and Khomeini came into office, only two students went back to Iran to support Khomeini. Within six months, they sent letters from Iran begging for help to come back to the United States. They said, "Khomeini was just a Shah with a turban around his head."

After the wedding, we stayed at the Holiday Inn and had dinner at the restaurant in Hobbs, New Mexico. This was not what we had planned for our honeymoon, but I was so sick. I asked Forrest if I could sleep until the food came. I was exhausted. I am a workaholic and did not know how to pace myself. I did not want any champagne to celebrate our wedding. We had the Bridal suite, but I just wanted to go to sleep.

The next day Forrest drove to Carlsbad while I slept. We were descending into Carlsbad when I told Forrest I was too sick. He took me home and then to the doctor. The doctor told me I needed to rest for six weeks. I was suffering "from exhaustion." I went home and went to bed and do not remember anything during that six weeks.

I don't love you because I need you. I need you because I love you.

Reflection Questions

1. Are you in a serious relationship?
2. Does this person know and understand God's call on your life?
3. Have you asked God if this relationship is right for you? He may have a better plan for you, something better than you ever imagined.

Action Steps

Begin your own journey toward trusting God for the person you are to marry. Read these scriptures and consider pre-marital counseling before you make this life-changing decision.

Read Genesis 2:24.

Define cleaving: _____

What does God mean when He says they will become one flesh? _____

Read Ephesians 5:21-31.

What are the roles of husband and wife according to the scriptures?

Why is following God's plan for marriage so important?

CHAPTER 8
VOYAGE OF DISCOVERY (1978-1980)

> *The voyage of discovery is not seeking*
> *new landscapes, but in having new eyes.*
> (Marcel Proust)

Forrest gradually brought his furnishings from the garage into our home. He did all the cooking, keeping the house, and taking care of me. No family members were there to assist. I knew he was a jewel. He set up his dark room during this time. He was a photographer by hobby even though he did some professional photography jobs for Houston Coca Cola Annual Sales meeting and took some pictures for Maytag Company to use during a legal suit against Maytag.

I slept so much, I do not remember much during this time. When I finally woke up, I was mad at myself for sleeping through our honeymoon. The timing to be exhausted was just awful. Well, that was the beginning of our great marriage! I suffered from exhaustion while I was working on a project with the Saudi Arabian Embassy. I think I have learned to pace myself now.

Prior to our marriage, Forrest asked me to promise to communicate even on little things, to not go to bed angry, and make sure we talk about such issues. Three months into our marriage, Forrest took many of his clothes to the cleaners at a cost of $41, and he was not working yet. That bothered me, but it was such a petty thing I did not say anything about it. Then, I felt guilty because I promised I would not go to bed angry so I became very quiet. He noticed I was tense, but did not say anything. We went to bed, but neither of us slept.

Finally, at 2:30 I popped up in bed and said, "I need to communicate."

That is the way it has been in our marriage.

Looking for a job in Lubbock, Texas is not like looking for a job in Houston. In Houston, with his technical skills he could leave one job in the morning and have another one that afternoon. Lubbock's industries were TTU, agriculture, and oil fields. Egypt was the number one producer of cotton and West Texas including Lubbock was the number two. Lubbock sits on top of a Cap rock overlooking all the naked arid and semi-arid land below with many tumbleweeds or Mesquite trees. Finally, Forrest got a job with a company that made cotton-stripper brushes.

I had asked Forrest to give me six months to adjust to having another person at home since I had been alone for so long. At the end of six months, I told Forrest, "Marriage has been fun. I have had no problem adjusting." He laughed and teased, "Jacquie, you have not been adjusting. I am the one who has done all of the adjustment. I resigned from my good job in Houston and had to find a new job in Lubbock. I left my home in Houston and moved to Lubbock." "Oh, Oh, of course," I admitted followed closely by an apology.

1979 – A Year of Surprises

One day someone from the Chinese Consulate in Houston called to invite me to be a member of a Fulbright Study Tour to visit Taiwan and many of its universities and to learn more about its educational system. The Taiwan Education Commissioner would host Forrest and me. I later learned that the Chinese Students Association at TTU nominated me. This was before the opening of the People's Republic of China. We stayed at the Grand Hotel in Taipei and took daily trips to various, impressive universities with excellent technology which Forrest thoroughly enjoyed.

Chinese students had told us to try some Dip Sum while we were there. Together with six other selected international educators who met us for breakfast that morning, we ordered twenty-seven different kinds and shared with one another. We ate too much. When we arrived at our 9:00 a.m. meeting, there were big cups of coffee, tall glasses of tea, a large slice of cake, and other goodies in front of each of our seats.

We looked at one another and wondered how we were going to eat another bite. We did to be polite. Then there was lunch hosted by the President of National Taiwan University which was a nine-course meal. Next was dinner hosted by the Education Commissioner, equivalent to our Secretary of Education in the United States. We paced ourselves through a nine-course meal, but five more courses of food were served. Forrest had never used chopsticks, but he gained eight pounds in a week using chopsticks. The hospitality in Taiwan was phenomenal.

Taiwan was in the process of building an East-West Highway across treacherous mountains with steep drop-offs. We rode on one narrow lane section from the East to the central part of Taiwan to have tea and lunch at the base of a beautiful pagoda. A man literally hung outside by hanging onto the front door of the bus to be sure the driver was keeping the wheels away from the edge of the cliff.

When Fred Bucy, President of Texas Instruments International (TII) and Chairman of the TTU Board of Regents at the time, learned that we had been invited to Taiwan, he invited us to visit the TI plants in Taipei and in Singapore which we did. One evening at 8:00 when we returned to the Grand Hotel, a limousine was waiting to take us to the Texas Instrument plant. The employees of the first shift were asked to stay over and show us the plant after which we were taken to dinner and did not get back to the hotel until midnight.

TI Employees demonstrating their technology to Jacquie

At the Singapore plant we dressed in white clothing, shoes, and hairnets to tour an area where one of the techs was looking at a screen that showed a two-macron hole in a piece of wire. The TI techs in Dallas also could see this. Amazing technology. Forrest loved it.

Being a computer techie, Forrest appreciated seeing all of the technology labs, computer equipment, and the Texas Instrument technology. Following Taiwan, China Airlines offered us a special to visit Singapore, Bangkok, and Hong Kong. This was an excellent opportunity for Forrest to be an active participant in international education. When we had a group of students for dinner at our home, I learned to put the techie group at a table in one room with Forrest and the non-techies with me in a separate room.

When I first moved to Lubbock, I had to sell my house in Houston and bought a small one in Lubbock. However, Forrest and I enjoyed having international students in our home and needed more space. We were fortunate to find a home with a large basement which was good to protect us from West Texas tornadoes and to host up to fifty students for a potluck.

We were moving into our new home on Labor Day weekend when Dr. Ewalt, the Vice President of Student Affairs, called to tell me a student had jumped off the Biology building. I went to the funeral home to identify him and then contacted the Ethiopian Embassy to get the appropriate documentation to go with his body back to Ethiopia.

Theo was from the Haile Selassi family that governed Ethiopia from 1930-1974. Holidays were tough for international students. I made contact with his father. It was tortuous for him to wait, but it took the Ethiopian Embassy two weeks to get the proper documents to me to accompany the body home.

In the mean time when TTU was back in session, a Memorial Service was held for Theo at the funeral home close to campus. There was a crowd in the funeral home, and people were lined up and down the street. A Coptic Orthodox priest from Houston performed the inspirational service. The father called to tell me that a service was planned for Theo, and the body must be back in a few days by noon. Fortunately, in mid-September, the papers came, and I was told that Theo arrived in Addis Ababa in time for the ceremony as people lined the street.

During this time, my nephew William Thomas was on the football team at Auburn University. He would be playing at Texas Christian University in Fort Worth, my alma mater, the following weekend. Forrest and I made the five-hour drive to Fort Worth to cheer for William. He told the coach his aunt was at the game. The coach called a play for William to catch a pass and he did! Auburn won! War Eagle!

During the fall semester, many international students were disturbed by Theo's death. Conversations now seemed to begin with, "Was he a Christian? Why are you a Christian?" I tried to explain it in a way they would understand, and then I would ask what they believed. Even at events and in our home, there were similar discussions. I left the initiation of the discussion up to the students.

At one gathering in our home, there was a discussion comparing what was in the Bible to the Qu'ran. There were Arab, Chinese, and Korean students at the table. Many Koreans were Christian, for the Baptist and especially the Presbyterians were strong in Korea.

One time a Buddhist student was describing his meditation until there was a stillness, peaceful feeling caused by "some strong force" as he referred to it. I asked if that could be God. He shrugged his shoulders. I did not push to convert, but I hoped our conversations piqued their interest and raised more questions. Sometimes they came back to ask more questions.

I had a big, colorfully jeweled butterfly ring. Sometimes to strike up a conversation, I would put the Butterfly Ring on my index finger, touch students on their shoulders, and say the butterfly brings you happiness. They got to the point they would come to the office for me to put my butterfly ring on their shoulders to bless them, especially on test day.

I was a hugger. Who else was going to hug them? Many were hurting inside. I prayed my actions spoke louder than my words. I think they knew I was a Christian and really cared for them regardless of their nationalities.

During the Iran-Iraq War, I vividly remember a young Iranian male student who came into my office. Finally, when he could compose himself, he told me his parents and siblings had escaped Iran and would be climbing over some mountain to go into Pakistan. He would not know for two weeks if they were safe or not. Many Iranian students had similar stories to tell. I wondered how they could even study under such pressure!

More Surprises in 1980

I had been selected by the National Association for Foreign Student Affairs (NAFSA) to be a member of a Fulbright Study Tour to Germany and Berlin to visit various universities and government administrative offices. At every site there was plenty to eat with beer on the table in the morning instead of tea, though I preferred water. I appreciated learning more about their educational system and think it has much merit. Even though we were guests of the German government, we had some trouble passing through the Berlin Wall into Berlin. We were finally authorized to visit universities there. There was an obvious difference in the face of the buildings and the demeanor of the people. I, for one, am glad that President Reagan said, "Tear down that Wall."

At the conclusion of my Fulbright tour and responsibilities, Forrest flew to Frankfurt and took the Eurail train to Hanover where he had traced the Behrens' genealogy. Then the plan was for him to meet me in Dusseldorf, Germany where we were to stay with one of my former students and her husband, who was the manager of the Mitsubishi operations in Europe.

However, all of Forrest's travel plans changed because Braniff Airline went bankrupt. Fortunately, Forrest got a flight to Germany, but it was earlier than his original plan. He got to Germany while I was still in Berlin. The hotel where I was supposed to be in Berlin had been changed. How did he find me?

God was with us, and we found each other in Hanover where he showed me Fritz Behren's Alley, a main thoroughfare with his uncle's name, and guided me around Hanover until it was time for us to go to Dusseldorf. My friend's husband had just returned from Russia and Spain.

We were fortunate that he could be in Dusseldorf while we were there. They took us to a sushi restaurant for our first meal. We had a wonderful visit with our special Japanese friends, Reiko and Kenichi Iwamoto.

Then we began our journey travelling by trains throughout Europe. We went first to Cologne, Germany to see the Gothic Cologne Cathedral. We took a cruise down the Rhine River enjoying the view of all of the castles on each side of the mountains.

We stopped at Frankfurt where I rented a locker at the airport and stored my Fulbright suits and shoes. I put on a pair of jeans and shirt and packed my backpack for the rest of the trip. Off we went to Heidelberg to visit the oldest university in Germany, then Munich Square where the Glockenspiel in the tower chimes, and on to the Neuschwanstein Castle which was the inspiration for the Disneyland Castle.

We loved riding the trains. We learned we should bring some fruit, cheese, bread, a knife, and a bottle opener for our meals or snacks on the train. The scenery of church steeples in the valleys was impressive. Everything was so clean. We had a grilled bratwurst from a vendor on the side of the road. It was delicious.

We learned to arrive in cities about 5:00 in the afternoon and walk around the city until we saw a sign for a room in someone's home to rent. One night about 8:00, we found a Zimmer Frei sign, meaning a room in a home is available to rent for the night. We knocked on the door. The owner came to the door and said she had a room, and did we want Vienna Schnitzel for dinner? We sat at a bench table with other couples from Belgium and France to watch the soccer game. The French and Belgium couples were cheering for Hamburg. Forrest and I cheered for Dusseldorf since we had just visited with our Japanese friends in Dusseldorf. We all spoke different languages, but we had fun.

Dallas was showing in Germany at the time, and they were anxiously waiting for the next show to see who killed J.R. We would not tell them.

From Germany, we went to Salzburg, Austria to visit Mozart's statue, and the Salzburg Castle/Fortress with walls surrounding it near where the Sound of Music was filmed on a hill overlooking Salzburg. Onward by train we went to Lucerne, Switzerland to see the Chapel Bridge and Water Tower over a major river at the end of Lake Lucerne. We ate at the local restaurants near the bridge where the dogs and cats laid under the table. We toured the United Nations Building in Switzerland, got disoriented, came out the wrong door, and missed the train to Lyon for dinner by one minute. We often would sleep on the train at night and set our alarm clock to ring ten minutes before we were to get off the train.

When we got on the trains to Italy, everything changed. The environment changed. In Germany everything was so clean, not so in Italy. The train was not on time, but we did make it to Venice in time to find a room and to find a Gondolier to take us for a Gondola ride to see Rialto Bridge and other bridges connecting one island to another. We enjoyed walking around Saint Mark's Square where people gathered to visit with one another. Unfortunately, Venice is gradually sinking, and there is not much they can do.

Our next stop was Rome, Saint Peter's Square, the Vatican, Saint Peter's Basilica, the Sistine Chapel with ceiling paintings by Michelangelo, and the residence of the Pope. Rome is the cradle of one of the world's greatest civilizations with so much influence throughout the world. There is the history of the Roman Coliseum, the Pantheon, Three Coins in the Fountain, and so much more. I was so relaxed. I wanted to keep on riding to Eastern European countries, but it was time to go back to work. We took the Eurail back to Frankfurt, picked up my suitcase, and flew back to the States.

Foster Parenting

As soon as we arrived home, we were called by the Adoption Agency. Forrest was thirty-five and I was thirty-seven so they were reluctant to give us a baby. The Agency had tried to force a teenager on us, but being an educator I knew the value of the first three years of a child's life and would not settle for a teenager. We would have to reeducate a teenager as to Christian values.

The Agency actually did not have many Caucasian babies who were free of addiction to alcohol, drugs or HIV. This was a puzzling stage in my life. Forrest and I would be loving parents to a child. We could afford a child and its needs. Why could we not have a child?

Forrest saw an advertisement on television about being Foster Parents. We attended Foster Parenting classes. We accepted Paul, a Mexican American baby, who had been in the hospital a month after his mother's boyfriend dipped him in hot, scalding water. He was burned from the waist down. We got Paul

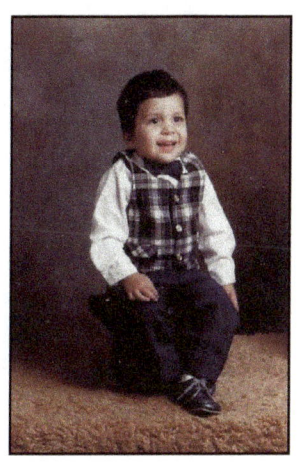
Paul, our precious foster child

and had to continue to treat him for burns. He was sixteen months old and precious. He had to relearn to talk.

Paul officially came into our lives in June. In a short time, he and Forrest were buddies. When Forrest took Paul to the babysitter in the morning, Forrest had his red cap on, his dark glasses, and carried a cup of coffee. Paul had his red cap on, his dark sunglasses, and carried a cup of milk. Forrest would meet him after work and bring him home.

Paul riding his horsey, Forrest

Forrest and I would cook supper, and Paul would play in the kitchen floor or at our kneecaps jabbering. He sat between us in his high chair during supper. He seemed so at peace with us. After dinner I washed the dishes and Forrest went to the den with Paul.

Paul immediately climbed into Forrest's lap and stayed there until we put him to bed. This went on for a month or so. We thought about making him get on the floor to play, but this baby had never had a loving man in his life. His father was in prison. Eventually, Forrest got onto the floor and played with him. Paul rode on Forrest's back and loved his horsey. Then he and Forrest played tackle on the floor.

On July 4, Forrest and I always attended a celebration cookout with friends. We were looking forward to taking Paul and sharing him with our friends. The Friday before the fourth, we took Paul to the doctor selected by the State of Texas to oversee Paul's health. Paul had fever.

As new foster parents we were concerned that we always did everything that needed to be done for Paul. The doctor gave us a prescription and said if Paul was not better by Sunday, we should bring him back in. We watched Paul's every move. His temperature remained over a 100 and seemed to be going up. By Sunday noon, he still had fever. We took him to the Emergency Room by 1:00.

It seemed as though we were in the Emergency Room forever. By this time, Paul was sitting up, no fever, and entertaining everyone royally. Nurses would come back in and play with Paul. He was laughing and having a grand time. We felt like fools. We brought him in lifeless with a fever, and now he was entertaining all the nurses.

Finally at 4:00, Dr. Fuqua came in and apologized for the wait. He said these nurses were on duty when Paul was brought in by his mother seventy-two hours after being dipped in hot, scalding water by her boyfriend. Dr. Fuqua and the nurses could not believe Paul was the same child who came in with all the burns. They had all wanted to see him.

Paul had a caseworker who picked him up from the sitter to take him to visit his mother once a week. The visits were not good. Paul continued to hit and reject her. After visiting with his mother, Paul was always hyper when he returned home in the evening, but relaxed as soon as he got into Forrest's lap.

He always favored Forrest who asked if this bothered me. I realized Paul had not had a loving male in his life. His mother had abused him, would not change his diaper, and never gave him any attention. He had to have temper tantrums to get his diapers changed. A female figure had not treated him well. When Paul and I were by ourselves, we were fine.

When we first got Paul, he had temper tantrums, usually while we were in the kitchen preparing dinner. Paul would sit on the floor and scream. We turned the stove off, went to another room until he stopped. We did not touch him, and he learned from our absence that he did not have an audience; thus, his temper tantrums were a waste. These lasted only about a week.

After two or three months of Paul having to visit with his mother, the caseworker brought Paul home to us. She told us Paul's mother' visits were being terminated. Paul just continued to hit her.

That same evening Paul was tense as usual. We sat down to eat with Paul between us, preparing to say our blessings. Paul reached out and took Forrest's hand and my hand. He put our hands to his face and pressed them to his face as he looked at us. To me this was his way of saying, "Thank You, I feel good here." This pause seemed to hang into eternity. I will never forget his touch and the love in his eyes! We then said our prayer of gratitude.

Prior to Paul's hospitalization, he had begun speaking in Spanish. With us, he was jabbering. My concern was if being in shock for seventy-two hours impaired his speaking capabilities. I knew his oxygen level was lower while he was in shock.

I made an appointment with an audiologist at Texas Tech University where I was working. He tested Paul and said he had all the speaking capabilities. Shortly after that Paul began speaking in English. Being with other children was good for him because his English continued to improve.

Later in the summer, his baby sitter went on vacation. We had to relocate Paul to another sitter for a week or two. The children were a little older than Paul and their vocabulary was a little different. Paul came home speaking more words. He seemed so happy. His demeanor was so peaceful and joyous.

One day after work, we all were in the den watching television when one of the case workers dropped by to check on Paul. She said there were other case workers in the car who had seen Paul prior to his being admitted in the hospital. She asked if they could come in to see Paul. They could not believe the difference. Paul knew he was the center of attention and entertained them for about thirty minutes.

Later, Forrest and I received the sad news that Paul's father had been released from prison and wanted Paul back. Later we learned after a short time Paul's father left him, but the good news was he was adopted by a young Mexican-American couple.

Reflection Questions

1. I prayed my actions spoke louder than my words. Do yours? Do people know you are a Christian by the way you treat others?
2. How do you treat people of other beliefs?

Action Steps

Jesus taught His disciples how to show others of God's love and then told them to go and witness to their world. As His modern day disciples, we have the same assignment. Read these examples of how Jesus trained His disciples and implement these methods in your own witnessing program.

John 13:34-35 says others will know we are disciples of Jesus by our _____

What did Jesus teach concerning little children in Matthew 19:13-15?

CHAPTER 9
LOOKING FORWARD, LOOKING BACKWARD (1981-1993)

> *No kind action ever stops with itself. One kind action leads to another....A single act of kindness throws out roots in all directions, and the roots spring up and make new trees. The greatest work that kindness does to others is that it makes them kind themselves. (Amelia Earhart)*

This chapter reviews some of the international programs in which I was involved.

Malaysia

Dr. Joe Neal, the Director of the International Office at the University of Texas and the President of the Texas

International Education Consortium (TIEC), contacted me about a project with the Malaysian Ministry of Education in Kuala Lumpur (KL). TIEC was a Consortium of thirty-two State universities in Texas. He requested I go with him to present TIEC's proposal to the Malaysian Ministry of Education. The plan was for TTU to be the lead university.

The Ministry wanted TIEC to locate a Texas university campus in KL at Shah Alam for 1600 Malaysian freshmen. These students would have to study English as a Second Language (ESL) prior to enrolling in the University courses. The Texas universities would have to provide the curricula and 200 faculty members to commit to teach in Malaysia for a year or more. TIEC committed.

This was a complicated project to implement. The curricula had to be approved by appropriate faculty members and deans. They also had to approve the faculty members to teach the courses in Malaysia. This process was very labor-intensive and time-consuming, but a **must** to maintain the Academic Integrity of the Texas universities and the students' relocation to Texas universities. The Bahasa Malay students had to go through the same severe screening as international students who applied for admission to a Texas university.

These students attended the Texas campus in Malaysia throughout their ESL and first two years of their general education courses. Then they were relocated to assigned universities in Texas. Over 200 architecture students, some engineering, and business students were relocated to Texas Tech, and about twenty TTU faculty members went to Kuala Lumpur to teach. Managing this program was one of the highlights of my years from 1984-2004.

I remember one day about twenty-five worried Malaysian students all came into my office together to say they failed their first project in Architecture. Their models looked different than the American student models. They were so sad. They had worked so hard.

I called the Dean of Architecture and asked him to meet with the students and me in the Exhibit room. We walked all the way across campus to see their projects. The Dean was very pleased with their projects. He told the students they were very creative, and their projects were excellent because they had injected their culture into their models.

In the fall of 1983, I learned I had to have surgery and be off work six months afterwards. I wanted to postpone the surgery because I had been approved to take leave from Texas Tech during the spring semester of 1984 to complete the course work in cross-cultural communication for my doctorate at the University of Texas at Austin.

The doctor would not postpone the surgery. Of course, Forrest agreed with the doctor. Fortunately, I was able to

Looking Forward, Looking Backward (1981-1993)

complete the Statistics course I was taking after I was home from the hospital. My dissertation topic was in the works. I was getting so close. Since I had been working with the Malaysian Ministry of Education, my research was to be a study of the reentry and reverse cultural shock for the 1600 Malaysians that were studying in Texas universities.

An official in the American Embassy in Kuala Lumpur had agreed to assist me in getting the data. Dr. Joe Neal was my international education mentor and my dissertation adviser. It was a perfect plan. This was a wonderful opportunity for me to further my career.

Why, God, do I have to have surgery now? Again, I did not understand God's timing to block me from completing my doctorate. I had worked so hard.

Jacquie and Dr. Joe Neal in Japan

Africa

The College of Agricultural and Natural Sciences at TTU often received students from the US Department of State Agency for International Development students, primarily from Africa. They were serious students and did well. One snowy January evening, Forrest and I met at the airport a group of students from Kenya, all handsome and dressed in their navy blue suits and white shirts. The Host Families sponsored a square dance and dinner for the incoming international students. Before I knew it they had me on the dance floor, dancing two steps to my one, and swinging me left and right. I was stepping on toes, and they were laughing and showing their snow white teeth.

Likewise, some American students wanted to work with Agency for International Development projects overseas. Therefore, with the cooperation of the Associate Dean William Bennett, we created an interdisciplinary course for both the Agency for International Development and the American students to prepare them to transition from one culture to another. This included budgetary issues, the lack of technology, and cultural adjustment upon returning home. In 1986, Dean Bennett and I compiled these lectures into a textbook titled, *Looking*

Forward, Looking Backward that was used throughout the United States, especially by the National Association of State Universities and Land Grant Colleges.

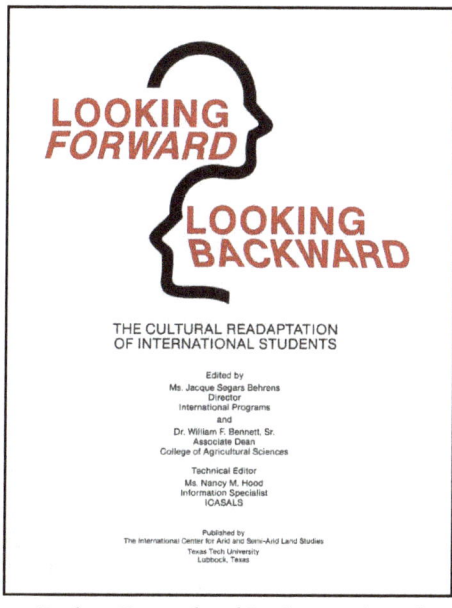

Looking Forward and Looking Backward

Peru

Partners of America was a program that came out of The World Alliance for Progress in 1961 under President Kennedy. It later became known as Partners for Americas. The purpose of this exchange was to facilitate a closer, cooperative effort to work together to improve the growth of the Latin American countries. Each state is matched with a partner in Latin America. Texas was matched with Peru, Veracruz, and Guerrero, Mexico. Alabama was matched with Guatemala.

Representatives from the Supreme Court of Peru had visited TTU and requested help with some of its medical issues. Dr. Nancy Ridenour, Associate Dean of Nursing from TTU's Allied Health and Medical School who spoke Spanish, accompanied me to Lima, Peru in 1986 during the Shining Path activities. The City was under curfew. We stayed in a fortress, literally, but we were secure. Dr. Ridenour got food poisoning. She was so sick.

We were accompanied by an Agency for International Development representative to tour a bald mountain in Lima with people scattered all over the mountain. They were without even cardboard housing. There was no electricity, water, or sanitation, and yet these women were having babies. Dr. Ridenour was concerned about how little we could do with no water or electricity. Flip charts in Spanish were suggested for Health Tips. Other health charts provided tips in Spanish on giving birth. This was the first step.

China

During the summer of 1988, I was selected to be a member of the Fulbright Hays Study Tour to China. At TTU, there is an International Center for Arid and Semiarid Land Studies (ICASALS) office that encompassed the interdisciplinary faculty members' participation in teaching, research, and service. Some of these faculty members were a part of this group.

A grant was received from the United States Department of Education to send sixteen members to the People's Republic of China to evaluate the infrastructure of China for its reliability for hosting an International Arid and Semiarid Conference. This Study Tour was a joint effort between the United States and the People's Republic of China.

The trip was rough. The bathrooms would gag a maggot. I remember staying in government housing at one stop, and the mop boy came in to clean the room. His mop reeked. It was never cleaned. It took a while for the stench to evaporate after he "cleaned." As more tourists have arrived in the People's Republic of China, I truly compliment China how much cleaner China was in 2000 than in 1988.

On another occasion, I remember a delegation from the People's Republic of China visiting me in my office. The People's Republic of China was opening up more and wanted to send Chinese students to TTU. I had a little flag from the Republic of China on Taiwan sitting on a stand on my book shelf. One of the officials pointed to the flag and stated something like we do not recognize that flag. My response was "I do not serve governments; I serve students from wherever they come".

United Arab Emirates

In 1995, I was selected as one of two females and fourteen men to be a Malone Fellow to the UAE which is comparable to the Fulbright program except this study tour is for countries only in the Gulf region of the Middle East. We visited all seven of the Emirates and all of the different Ministries to learn about services available to Emiratis. We were always served tea with cardamom. I liked the tea!

Looking Forward, Looking Backward (1981-1993)

Malone Fellows visit to one of the Ministries

Jacquie enjoying tea being served

A highlight of this tour was a trip via a C-30 over the Straits of Hormuz which was only about twenty-six miles. Thirteen miles are over Omani waters and thirteen miles are over Iranian waters. For miles and miles, we could see freighters lined up to go through the Straits of Hormuz in the Omani waters.

Jacquie in the C-30 flying over the Straits of Hormuz

TTU and Japan

In 1989, TIEC was invited to put a Texas campus in Yamagata Prefecture on the Western side of Japan by the Sea of Japan. Dr. Joe Neal invited Dr. Donald Haragan, Executive Vice President and Provost at TTU, and me to accompany him to Japan to evaluate this request and the resources available to us. The proposal was for Texas Tech to be the lead University.

A government official of the Japanese Parliament equivalent to a U.S. Senator met us at the Narita Airport and escorted us to a grand dinner with several officials.

Looking Forward, Looking Backward (1981-1993)

We were all so tired; we just wanted to go to bed after a thirteen-hour flight.

The next day, the Japanese official helped us transfer from the hotel to the train station. One whole train car was reserved just for the four of us. The seats were covered in pressed cotton covers, and hors d'oeuvres were available. The train ride to the Eastern side of Japan by the Sea of Japan showed us the beautiful country landscape. Upon arrival, we were shown the property chosen for the Texas Tech campus.

All of the revenue for building the campus, the operation of the campus, and the academic programs would be provided by Yamagata Prefecture. TTU deans would identify the curricula and select faculty. After the students completed their ESL and first two years at Yamagata, I would assist in relocating the students to universities in Texas. Now we had to evaluate all Yamagata was offering.

Also, Dr. Haragan and I were invited to visit a friend of TTU who lived in Kyoto. We took the Shinkansen, the fast train in Japan, from Tokyo to Kyoto. Kyoto is the cultural capital of Japan that is home to the ancient Imperial Palace, the Heian Shrine, Gold and Silver Pavilions, and beautiful Japanese Gardens. Abe San hosted us in a teahouse for a delicious Japanese meal that was served by a Geisha with all the formality and ritual to make our time together exquisite. That was one of my favorite memories.

When I knew Dr. Haragan and I would be going to Japan, I contacted some of our alumni and told them on what dates we would be in Tokyo, and that we would like to schedule a time to meet them. One significant response was from a 1965 alumnus who invited us for dinner at his home. Dr. Haragan and I took the Shinkansen from Kyoto to Tokyo and were rather tired. However, we needed to get ready to meet Saito san as he was scheduled to pick us up at 6:00. He had just arrived back to Tokyo himself from Bangkok.

We were standing outside the hotel when a Mercedes Benz pulled up to the door, and Saito San got out of the car and greeted us. Dr. Haragan and I got into the back seat, and Saito san sat upfront with the driver who wore white gloves. We wove through the traffic of downtown Tokyo and arrived at a location where we drove up a long driveway to his home.

I had never seen a home this big in Japan except for the Imperial Palace. The butler met us at the front steps and showed us a large fish that he said Kobayashi Sensei had brought for dinner. We later learned that Kobayashi Sensei was a renowned Japanese educator who was invited to explore the Texas proposal with us. This was a pleasant surprise.

First, we were escorted to a waiting area and served a drink. Then Saito San escorted us to his wine cellar in the basement. He was a collector of wines from around the world. Dr. Haragan and I sat on the floor at a low table and were served some raw fish and some of his valuable wine. Saito San explained that his family is the one that started exporting Green Tea. This palatial home in the middle of Tokyo was 411 years old in 1989.

We were then escorted to a long room overlooking the beautifully manicured Japanese gardens that were absolutely gorgeous. We were seated at a long, low table with about twenty other people. He seated Kobayashi Sensei next to Dr. Haragan and me next to Dr. Haragan. Saito san sat next to Kobayashi Sensei. Kobayashi Sensei and Dr. Haragan were the honored guests. We were served an appetizer, a large prime rib, then a whole lobster on each plate, and the fish that Kobayashi Sensei had brought along plus soups and fruit. We ate from 7:00 p.m. until 1:00 a.m.

During this time, I was asked to describe the proposal. I presented the proposal, and then Dr. Haragan spoke from the Texas Tech perspective. Kobayashi Sensei asked some very good thought-provoking questions and then advised Texas Tech not to participate in this venture. He stated there were not enough students in the pipeline in Japan for a campus like this to succeed. The Government was pursuing us, yet Kobayashi Sensei seemed to understand the situation better. This is a very special memory!

When I retired from TTU, Dr. Haragan spoke at my retirement reception. One statement he made was that "Jacquie saved the University a lot of money". Other universities in Texas, Oklahoma, and other states had to close their campuses in Japan.

Saito San and Jacquie San observing tea ceremony

I visited Saito San several times when I went to Japan. The last time, he advised me to meet him at the Country Club in downtown Tokyo. When he arrived, we were escorted to a tea house in the middle of the gardens. A special chef arrived and prepared our delicious meal in front of us. Then a Tea Master came to perform a Tea Ceremony with us. During this time, I learned that the annual membership fee in this Club was a million dollars a year.

This man was amazing. My dream was for TTU to establish a Tea Center at the University in honor of him. I had the property selected. Unfortunately, he died during the economic crises in Asia about 1997. He was developing new resort areas in New Zealand at the time.

Reflection Questions

Have you ever asked God why He is doing some particular thing in your life?

Did you find out afterwards the reason?

Action Steps

As you continue your own journey toward trusting God's ways and His timing in your life, remember these important truths.

2 Samuel 22:31 says, _____

Psalm 37:5-6 tells you to _____ and promises _____

CHAPTER 10
CLIMB EVERY MOUNTAIN UNTIL YOU FIND YOUR DREAM (1994-2003)

KnASTU and KnA Oil Refinery

In 1994, many people still considered Russia the enemy or at least far too different for Americans to collaborate with. However, while sitting at my desk at TTU, I received a phone call from Komsomolsk-na-Amur (KnA) in Far East Russia, known as Siberia, asking if a delegation could visit TTU to establish a partnership in a project. In the early summer months of 1995, Leonid Razvozzhaev, Chief of the KnA Oil Refinery, Dr. Kabaldin, President of the KnA State Technical University (KnASTU), and Grennady Usanov, faculty member in international education and Luda, the translator, arrived. They had an idea, but were not sure how to implement it and did not understand the American educational system. The KnA Oil Refinery wanted help in educating some of the Russian boys at KnASTU at TTU in Chemical Engineering. The Refinery had identified a particular module that it wanted to purchase from the States so that the Refinery could refine its oil into gas and wanted the students to be educated at TTU so they could assist in this endeavor. They stayed for a week while we hammered out an Agreement in Russian and English; and they returned to KnA to prepare ten boys to enroll at TTU in the fall of 1995.

Russian delegation and Jacquie drafting agreement between TTU, KnASTU, and KnA Oil Refinery.

Ten students arrived. Forrest and I were at the airport to meet them. They were to study ESL first and then go into Chemical Engineering (CE) as juniors. The CE Chair and faculty were diligent in evaluating the level of the courses taken in Russia and how they compared them to the equivalences of courses at TTU. Since Russian students had not been coming to American universities, we really did not know how to compare their academic courses. The CE faculty members were most pleased with the technical talent of these ten students. In fact, the CE Chair told the KnA Oil Refinery Chief and the KnASTU President when they visited again not to send any more students in engineering. They should send students to study business.

The next fifteen students took business courses and did well. Some of the CE students advanced to masters and doctorate degrees. These students were so young and naïve about the American ways and did not have good command of English. Yet during their first Christmas holidays, they rented two cars, with one group going to New York and another to Disney World in Florida. They must have sensed my anxiety, for on Christmas Eve I received two phone calls, one from New York and one from Florida. They were doing fine and having a great time. New Years' Eve, I received two more calls. Because of

In Loco Parentis, I could not act as a parent to University students, but most of the international students thought of me otherwise. They were hungry for "family" so we fed them the only way we knew how-we loved them.

Russian students watching Men in Black at our home

Shortly thereafter, the Dean of Engineering and I were invited to visit KnA. We flew via Anchorage to Khabarovsk, and then took a hydrofoil boat the next morning for a six-hour ride up the KnA River to KnA. Many were at the harbor to welcome us. We stayed in a house that the Refinery must have rented for us. There were no hotels in KnA with a population of 100,000. We visited the Refinery, the University, and the Gargarin (name of first Russian cosmonaut) Air Construction Factory that was no longer making military planes after

Yeltsin's transition from communism. Many factories closed because the government no longer supported them financially nor bought their products. The Gargarin instead was making recreational boats, bicycles, and tricycles. The factory that made the KnA submarines was now making furniture. This was a tough transition for Russians, though the Oil Refinery was doing okay because it was the biggest one in the Far East.

Jacquie's business card in English and Russian

The Russian hosts asked if I would speak to 500 elementary children. Fortunately, I had read some of the Russian folk tales that were comparable to ours in America. I told the fairy tale about the Prince and the Frog and asked if they knew that story. They were all so excited for that was their folk tale, too. These precious children had never seen an American and they all wanted to touch me.

Jacquie telling frog to prince folktale to children

On our return trip to the States, the Dean and I were stuck in Khabarovsk for three days because the plane did not make it in. We would have to wait as the airplane only flew in on Saturday and Tuesday. The partnership between

TTU and KnA was a big success from 1995-2004. Forrest and I considered Dr. Kabaldin, Leonid, and Grennady as friends after our many visits together. Sometimes I cooked for them and sometimes we went out to eat. One year they were at our home during Thanksgiving, and I cooked turkey and dressing. I could not believe my eyes. Leonid put hot sauce on my turkey and dressing and drank straight whiskey with dinner.

> **We were different; but as we took the time to get to know them, we found we also had many similarities.**

As an international educator, patience and flexibility are requirements. During another visit Dr. Kabaldin, Leonid, and Grennady asked Forrest to take them shopping to get something for their wives. We had lived in Lubbock for seventeen years, but Forrest did not know where a dress shop was. I do not know if he had ever been to the Mall. They went to the Mall and looked for a dress store. They walked into one and asked for a 44 or 46 dress size, but our sizes in the States are different from other countries. They were not getting too far with this, and they were miserable shopping in this store anyway. Forrest suggested they buy cosmetics for their wives.

Then all of these men packed into a small Rav 4 and went to buy electronics. They had no translator with them, but Forrest could help them in purchasing electronics. They had fun together. Luda, the translator, and I drove to Walmart in my Cadillac. She was so overwhelmed with so much to buy in this store that she could not decide what to buy. She finally bought a cap.

On another occasion, this delegation came, and I scheduled meetings for them and arranged dinner plans with faculty of ESL or CE. They cancelled all of their dinner schedules. Later, I learned their Embassy Suites Hotel was next to an Albertson's Grocery store. They liked to go buy their food and then Marina, the translator, cooked for them. They were having a blast shopping in the American grocery store.

The European Association of International Education (EAIE) was hosting its conference in Budapest, Hungary. I was invited to co-host a session with a Hungarian telecommunication faculty member. The multicultural class that I taught in the TTU College of Education participated in a telecommunication contest and was recognized as honorable mention. The TTU students communicated with students from around the world to learn about other cultures. Margie Kidd, the Director of the International Office at the University of Texas at Austin, and I attended this conference. During our free time, we took a trolley car to see Budapest at night. Unfortunately, the trolley had made its last run, and we ended up in the overnight trolley parking lot in the middle of nowhere. Somehow we got back into the city and took another trolley.

Budapest is one of my favorite cities. The beauty of the Parliament mirrors itself in the Danube River. God was still giving me many opportunities to see faraway places with strange- sounding names!

On my way home, I called my office from the Houston airport to learn that one of the Russian students, Vitaly, had died in a car accident. I rushed from the Lubbock airport to the funeral home and called the Russian Embassy for appropriate documentation. I made all the funeral arrangements, but I did not know what different colors and numbers meant in Russia. I called for advice and had an arrangement made with the proper number of white flowers to place on the casket. The other boys called KnASTU and their parents who notified Vitaly's parents.

All of the Russian students and their American friends brought red roses and placed them in the casket at the Memorial Service. When the Service was over, the boys continued to sit there. I motioned for them to get up. They did not. Finally, the audience departed the room, but stayed in the lobby waiting for the boys.The funeral director needed to put the casket in the hearse to take to the airport in time to meet the plane.

The attendants started preparing the casket inside to let the lid down. The boys stepped in because they had to do something for their friend. They helped carry the casket to the hearse and followed it to the airport. I appreciate how the attendants allowed the boys to do what they had to do according to their culture. One of the students accompanied the body back to KnA. In spite of In Loco Parentis, their parents unofficially made Forrest and me their guardian parents while they were at TTU. We had become part of these twenty-five students and their parents' lives. We all shared in making these students successful.

In October, I was invited to represent Dr. Magne Kristiansen, an outstanding, scholarly faculty member in the TTU Electrical Engineering department who was known for his research for pulsed power, to a major pulsed power conference at Kumamoto University in Japan. I was out of my league. All these men were scientific scholars, but were very accepting of my questions. This was a good experience.

The host at Kumamoto was Dr. Hidenori Akiyama who started his career as a post doctorate student in Dr. Kristiansen's lab. His operation is the second largest university laboratory in the world in this field after TTU. What is unique about his laboratory is that it is almost exclusively devoted to non-military topics. Dr. Akiyama used pulsed power with algae projects.

I was enthralled to learn how their research was so intertwined. Dr. and Mrs. Gennady Mesyats were there. Dr. Mesyats, the Senior Vice President for the Russian Academy of Sciences, had visited TTU to work with Dr. Kristiansen. I enjoyed having the opportunity to visit with him again.

Pulsed Power Conference l-r Jacquie Behrens, University President, Dr. Mesyats of the Russian Academy of Sciences, Dr. Akiyama, host.

The Russian students must have told someone who told the new Chief of the KnA Oil Refinery that I would be in Japan in October. The new Chief stated he would pay my way to visit KnA. I made the trek from Japan to

KnA again. During my five-minute meeting with the new Chief of the Refinery, he barely welcomed me.

He stated very firmly, "TTU is not to admit any more KnA students for graduate work nor give them any scholarships. When the students finish their bachelor's, you are to send them home."

I responded, "TTU will not do this. It is the Oil Refinery who has a contract with these students, not TTU."

He then told me, "Tell the President of TTU what I have said and have him write me a letter agreeing to my demands."

He stood up and walked away. After my five-minute meeting, the parents of the students invited me to a picnic on the KnA River, the ninth longest river in the world that was half frozen over. The parents were so thoughtful. Knowing I was from the semi-arid desert climate, they brought me a toboggan knit hat, scarves for my neck, vests, sweater, mittens, socks, boots, and coat. They were surprised I had a coat on.

We picnicked in the woods next to the frozen river. None of them spoke English, and mine was limited to "Spicebo - Thank You." We played charades frequently and laughed at ourselves. The parents pointed to a log for me to sit on. The mothers brought out all of their pickled foods from their summer gardens. The men put on

Russian music and came over for me to dance with them. I could hardly dance; I had so many clothes on, and there were so many holes in the ground.

They were just happy to be with someone who was close to their sons. They had already heard what the new Chief of the Oil Refinery had told me. I told them TTU would not do as he demanded. I seriously thought he might be playing Russian and just bluffing, but this was the first time I ever met this man. He was not like Leonid at all.

When I arrived back to TTU, I met with President Haragan to give him the message, and he said, "Jacquie, write a letter for me saying exactly what you told him, and I will sign it."

I met with the students as well and expressed concern, and they said, "Oh, Jacquie, do not worry about it. He was just bluffing."

I thought this was the case, but I still felt the need to tell the students.

The students said, "In Russia, when someone is given a title, he has authority. In America, a person may be given a title, but there are checks and balances in place."

The President's letter was mailed, and TTU received more money from the refinery for the students' tuition.

The International Cultural Center – **Another dream**

In working with international students, one of my biggest challenges was to facilitate activities to get American students to interact with international students. Intramural sports were good. Having language partners was good so international students could speak English with American students, but these relationships did not carry over to other activities. My thinking was maybe if TTU had an international house, there would be more interaction. Also, my thought was to add international programs for K-12 school children to pique their interest in other cultures and the necessity of learning another language. Every high school and college student must be globally competent to participate in the global economy and at the peace table. Banks all along the Mexican border with Texas were seeking bilingual students in Spanish and business.

In 1978, I met with the Host Families Board and suggested we needed an International House for both American and international students. This house also needed to offer K-12 international education programs to supplement their studies. Each one agreed this would be great, but that was as far as it went.

In the mid-80's I was flying out of Lubbock, Texas to visit a college campus with an international house. The editor of the Lubbock Avalanche Journal, our local newspaper, was on this flight and asked where I was going. I told him my dream for an international house for students and K-12 international educational programs to supplement their curricula in school. He was on his way to Turkey and said he would contact me when he returned. He did.

We established a board of community leaders, bankers, lawyers, an architecture professor, and me. I outlined my dream for an International Cultural Center (ICC) to the Board. We needed to raise money. In time we had raised two million dollars, but we needed three million, plus we needed money to hire a teacher to prepare programs representative of different countries/cultures.

Senator John Montford from Lubbock, Chairman of the State Finance Committee, learned about the ICC dream. He informed the ICC Board that every two years the Texas Legislature designated money to special projects at state universities. Of course, much of this money had gone to the University of Texas at Austin and Texas A & M University. He submitted the TTU proposal to the finance committee, and TTU was awarded three million dollars to build the ICC. The two million we raised could now be used to develop programs for K-12 children.

I was one of the board members to propose a design for the ICC.

l-r J Harris, Editor of Lubbock Avalanche Journal; Jacquie Behrens; Rev. Dudley Strain, Chairman of the Board; and George Peng, TTU Architecture Professor. Drafting a design for the ICC.

Ground-breaking ceremony for ICC

Climb Every Mountain Until You Find Your Dream (1994-2003)

Exterior of International Cultural Center

There were sixty school districts in West Texas. Many of these schools agreed to use their buses to transport the students to the ICC and to pay $.25 cents for each child that visited the Center. The ICC was completed in 1997, nineteen years after the birth of an idea. The Center was managed under the umbrella of the Office of International Affairs. We had programs that assimilated the students' arrival as immigrants to Ellis Island requiring students to have passports and visas to the States. They had to meet Nurse Raschit who prevented some of the children from entering because of some health issue; some were denied because they could not say a tongue twister correctly, thus denied because of their lack of English skills.

There were programs on the Amazon Jungle, Japanese Sakura dance, the Peruvian rain coat made completely of straw, and so many more programs. The students had to see on the big globe in the Center of ICC the location in the world they would be visiting each time they came. Two Russian dancers arrived from California. The female dancer got all the little girls on stage and taught them how to dance a Russian dance. The boys were in the auditorium laughing at the girls. Then the male dancer jumped up on stage and invited all of the boys onto the stage. The Russian music started playing, and he taught them how to do the squat dance and kicking out their legs in front. It was hilarious and exhausting to the boys, and they did not say a word when they got back to their seats.

There were new programs every month. My dream was that when these K-12 children went to college, they would have remained curious enough to learn a second language. TTU taught them all Arabic, Chinese, French, German, Japanese, Spanish, and other languages as well. I would like to see some research that followed the education of the students who visited the Center and what percentage went on to study a second language.

Reconnecting with Former Students –
a wonderful reward

In 2000, I was no longer Director of International Education. The division was split into three areas with three directors: International Students and Scholars, Study Abroad, and I became the Director of the new division - International Institutional Advancement, International Alumni, and International Recruitment. This meant that I would be travelling more overseas to meet with alumni who were students in the 70's, 80's, and 90's in my earlier years at TTU. It was great to reunite with them and see them as adult leaders in their careers.

As I visited with alumni in Korea, one lady came to me to say, "Jacquie, do you remember me when I came into your office with a big problem? I remember everything you told me. I am okay now. You had on a green dress."

Yes, I remembered her and her problem, not the green dress.

Another beautiful, smiling lady came up to me and said, "Are you the same Jacquie that wrote a letter supporting me for a PEO scholarship?"

I wondered how many letters I wrote, how many phone calls I made, and how many students I counseled. I remember getting up at 3:00 in the morning for a week to call the American Embassy in Nairobi on behalf of a student's need. Often when I finally got home at night, I would think I did not get anything done today because I did not get a brochure written, work done on budget or other administrative issues. After seeing these alumni and learning my impact of their visits with me, I thanked God that I had my priorities right by visiting with students and the decisions that were made during these sessions.

One of the former doctoral students in economics was the Mayor during my last visit in 2001 of a town along the Western military demarcation line between North and South Korea. On this particular trip, I also visited with alumni in Japan, China, Taiwan, Singapore, Indonesia, and Malaysia. These visits were very humbling as the students talked about their deep love for TTU, the International Office, the counselors, and their professors.

It overwhelmed me how much we impacted their lives as they matured to be leaders in their societies and spreading the influence of TTU on their lives – another example of the roots of the tree that continue to spread and produce new trees. One student from China who got his doctorate from TTU put the internet backbone into China with the full support of the People's Republic of China President and the Chinese Academy of Science. Ed

Climb Every Mountain Until You Find Your Dream (1994-2003)

Tian and his wife have been visitors in our home in Lubbock and I in their home several times in Beijing.

My alumni and recruitment visits continued to Costa Rica, El Salvador, Honduras, and Mexico. It was fun to meet one of the alumni in Honduras who even had his beanie cap from his freshmen orientation at TTU in the 50's. He still laughed about the panty raids. Another TTU architectural alumnus hosted a dinner on the patio of his home that was built on top of a mountain overlooking the Tegucigalpa Valley ringed by forested trees. It was amazing how deep their love was for TTU. Again I am reminded -

Jacquie and Ed Tian in Beijing

No kind action ever stops with itself. One kind action leads to another. A single act of kindness throws out roots in all directions, and roots spring up and make new trees.
-Amelia Earhart

Reflection Questions

We may have different cultures, but if we look hard enough we can see that we also have many similarities. An international educator needs patience and flexibility, but so do all of the disciples of Jesus if we are going to be effective in fulfilling our great commission assignment.

Would people define you as patient and flexible?

Are you willing to take the time to find out the things you have in common with those of different cultures and beliefs within the United States?

Action Steps

Continue your own journey toward fulfilling your assignment from God. Read these verses and meditate on how important it is for you to be patient and flexible when it comes to being an effective witness for Jesus. Read Mark 16:15-20. What is your assignment? _____

_____

Realize going into all the world can also mean reaching out to others in your own neighborhood and community. Research your area and perhaps attend a multi-cultural local event to meet others from varying cultures. Remember to honor their beliefs and exhibit God's love through your own patience and flexibility.

In my own life, the Russians were considered the enemy. Read Proverbs 25:21-22.

Explain these verses in your own words.

How can you implement this principle in your own life?

I had a big dream for an international cultural center to teach students and K-12 through international educational programs to supplement their curricula in school. God sent the people needed to fulfill this dream.

What dream has God given you for reaching people with His love?

CHAPTER 11
LIFE'S ROLLER COASTER (2003-2014)

> *The next time you run into a bit of grief, remember that many a man has bitten into an overripe oyster and found himself chewing on a pearl.* (Unknown)

Life was a roller coaster starting in 2003 even with God beside us. There was a reason, but I did not know it then. Forrest had two surgeries to repair both of his rotator cuffs, the last one being March 2003. In May, Forrest and I both decided we would work another ten years. In the meantime, we refinanced our home so that it would be paid in full when we retired. Also in May, we planned to visit Decatur in late October to spend three days to visit Mother, two days to complete a consultation with the international office at UNA, and three days to drive with Mother in tow to North of Chattanooga to look at eleven acres that we were considering for retirement.

We closed on refinancing our home on July 15, And rushed Forrest in an ambulance to the ER. It was determined he had a collapsed left lung. A pulmonary surgery team was pulled together about two o'clock in the morning to operate. Forrest was in surgery for a long time. Finally the doctor came in to say the surgery went well, and he would be moved to ICU.

Forrest was the director of the TTU Computer Store so I called to give an update on the surgery. Some of the student workers must have gone around the store collecting goodies to bring to me in the Waiting Room. They brought pretzels, candy, soda, and waited with me until Forrest was finally moved to ICU. I could see Forrest briefly, but then had to leave.

These students loved Forrest and knew he cared. Instead of having lunch with their friends, most of the student employees gathered around a table in the computer store where Forrest was eating and enjoyed all the merriment during lunch. When it was work time, they were hard workers and wanted to learn more about computers.

Forrest was in ICU for over a week. One day, I was sitting with Forrest in ICU when a group of cardiologists came in to tell me he had a heart attack on the operating table. They told me as soon as Forrest's lung cavity had drained all of the bronchitis infection, he would have to have heart surgery. In August Forrest had heart surgery. Once he was safely back in ICU, I went to the office.

I had received an email saying I had been selected as one of three Americans to consult with three Koreans, three Japanese, and three Europeans in developing an International Model. We would meet in Prague on September 15, for five days to develop our model, and then travel to Vienna, Austria to present it at the European Association for International Education Conference. This was an honor, but I did not think I could go.

I talked to the doctor at length and asked how long Forrest would be in the hospital and what his care would require after he got home. I explained to the doctor about the possible trip, and the doctor encouraged me to plan to go because Forrest would just need time to rest. As Forrest was about to go home, I asked him about the trip. As always, he encouraged me to go. I went, but Forrest did not do as well as the cardiologist led me to believe. I called Forrest every night and could not wait to get home.

Dr. Josef Mestenhausen, a Czech himself, was the leader of this group. He was the former director of the international office at the University of Minnesota, and at the time of this trip was the Czech Consul General in Minneapolis. He and I had dinner in the Old Town Square below the St. Vitus Cathedral one evening, and afterwards we walked around the Square and across St. Charles Bridge. He reflected on the time he was a participant in the numerous protests in Prague during his college days and was even imprisoned. This was a memorable evening with Dr. Mestenhauser telling of his trials and tribulations as we walked back in history when there was such turmoil.

As soon as I got back home, Forrest and I went to see his cardiologist and pulmonologist. Both physicians told Forrest he should quit work immediately, or he would be dead within three years. This was a bombshell! Forrest, being a he-man thought he could work, but he was chewing up the nitro tablets.

Forrest and I had airline tickets to Florence for October 30, 2003, for my consultation at the UNA International Office. However, Friday, October 10, my sister called to say Mother had been rushed to the Huntsville Hospital from Assisted Living with a directive to the physician to not resuscitate. The doctors had resuscitated Mother even though she had a major stroke and was unconscious. I was on the next flight to Huntsville and arrived at the hospital at 6:00 p.m.

I asked to see the doctors and was told they had gone home. I requested that the doctors come back and remove the life support. The doctors returned about 6:45 and removed the life support. Nothing happened. The doctor who came in Sunday morning told me Mother would not die soon as she had been given enough medication to keep her alive for seven days.

I flew back to Lubbock because Forrest was not well. The next Saturday morning at 4:00 a.m., Patsy called to tell me Mother had died. I returned home for my final farewell to my precious Mother. *Well done thy good and faithful servant of God and a rock for our family.*

October 30, Forrest and I flew to Huntsville and drove on to Florence. Within six months, God had changed everything. First, Forrest's health issues had changed any plans of our retiring in Tennessee. I did not want to live in the mountains of Tennessee by myself. Secondly, we had planned to spend three days with Mother and take her with us to Tennessee. She died October 18.

This was a tortuous trip for Forrest. Some of his ribs were broken and the nerve endings were coming alive. Nobody told him they broke his ribs to take his heart and lungs out of his chest. I will never forget Van Morgan for packing pillows in the back seat of his SUV to cushion the bumps while showing us around Florence which is at the base of the Appalachian Mountains and on the Mighty Tennessee River. We were amazed at how tall the trees were, how much grass there was, and how beautiful the flowers were.

Forrest made the statement, "I could retire here."

This was music to my ears, for I certainly did not want to return to Chicago. We had seven days to see Florence and visit with family in Huntsville. Florence had not even been on our radar screen; however, our visit determined that we would retire in Florence. We had not accepted the fact that we would be retiring and moving this very year.

Forrest and I agreed that since we were here we should contact a real estate agent to show us what houses were like in the area. Notice that God made room for enough time for us to look at houses even though we had not committed to retirement. We went from house to house all of one day. Forrest did not get out of the car, but he could see the area and the exterior of the house.

At the end of the day, I said I would like to go back and see the first house we toured. When we revisited it in the afternoon, I realized it had a creek behind it and a bluff on the other side of the creek. I liked the inside of the house, too. Forrest did come into this last house since I was looking at it twice, and he did not have to climb any stairs.

By December, Forrest decided he could not work much longer. December 23, Forrest received a phone call from Spears Furniture saying, "Mr. Behrens has won $10,000 of furniture." I screamed. Forrest woke up and told me to go to Spears and see what furniture he wanted and get him the biggest TV they had. Spears did not sell televisions so I picked out a master bedroom suite. I woke up that morning thinking about the house in Florence. We did not have bedroom furniture for one of the rooms.

Forrest said, "It seems God is pushing us to Florence."

We put our house in Lubbock up for sale even though it was a terrible time of the year to try to sell a house. We put a contract down on the house we liked in Florence, but the owners did not accept our offer. In March, we got a contract on our house in Lubbock. We made an offer on the house in Florence again. The owners rejected it again and the contract on the Lubbock house was withdrawn when the couple decided to build. In April, we got another contract on our Lubbock home, and we submitted the same contract on the same house with the statement, we were moving to Florence, May 4, and we are buying a house. The owner finally accepted our offer.

If God brings you to it; He will see you through it.

We both had good jobs. Forrest was the director of the TTU computer store, and I was the director of the International Institutional Advancement, Alumni, and Recruitment of International Students to TTU. We both had to leave our comfort zones and retire at the base of the Appalachian Mountains on the mighty Tennessee River with three dams within fifty miles of our home on Cypress Creek. We did not want to retire, but this seemed to be God's plan. We had a tsunami of emotions and were exhausted by the time we got to Florence. God made arrangements in October for us to have time to look at houses while we were in Florence because He knew we would eventually have to decide to retire there.

God Knew Exactly What We Needed

We could not have done any better in pursuing a retirement home if we had searched the world over. There are many tall Red Oak trees surrounding our home. When we sit on the deck, we feel like we are in a tree house celebrating the budding of spring trees with fresh lime leaves, colorful tulips, daffodils, chirping birds with their babies, the babbling creek with a Blue Heron spreading its wings as it flies to its nest, and the pesky little squirrels and chipmunks chasing one another in the backyard.

Recently, I saw a little red fox chasing a ground hog to the creek, and one day we watched as a turtle crawled toward the house to lay its eggs. This scenery was perfect in helping us to relax from the stress of the surgeries.

Forrest was now officially disabled and could not work. Adding to our retirement fund had been cut short by twenty years. I needed to work. I was sixty-one so who would hire me? I had worked for thirty-five years and loved every minute of my career. My dream of building the new division that TTU had created for me to visit with alumni, recruit, and counsel international students was over. Now, we had to start a new life.

> **Pat Conroy once said, "Once you have traveled, the voyage never ends, but is played out over and over again in the quiet chambers. The mind can never break off from the journey."**

This was my state of mind. I was thinking the glass was half empty instead of half full. I was having a "pity party." My mind rushed to the time Mother had rushed Patsy to the Emergency Room. Mother had been having a "pity party" because she could only buy us one pair of shoes a year until she looked around the Emergency

Room and saw a man with a little girl who had no feet. My "pity party" was over. I started counting my blessings. Forrest was alive. We had each other. We were safe, had food, and were warm in our home.

I prayed and asked God for strength and courage to find a job. As usual, God had a plan that was much better than I could have ever imagined. I should have learned not to depend on me.

When we arrived in Florence, my reputation had preceded me as a result of my consultation to the international office in 2003. I was elected to serve on the University of North Alabama National Alumni Board. Then I was invited to meet with the new President, Dr. William Cale. He asked if I would accept a three-year contract as Director of International Recruiting in the international office during this transition time. I was re-energized again. I had worth again. I had confidence again. God had a plan much better than mine. He was not finished with me yet.

Reflection Questions

1. Have you ever been so ready to complete a project/program and then have to stop after you have put so much effort into it?

2. What has God done in your life to show you His plans are different than yours?

Action Steps

Continue your own journey toward trusting God during the good times and bad, meditate on His promises even when you do not understand why certain things are happening in your life

Read Romans 8:28. What is this verse saying to you today?

Read Romans 8:37-39. What are the amazing promises God has given you in these verses?

CHAPTER 12
GOD IS NOT FINISHED WITH ME YET (2004-2015)

During those three years I became a senior citizen globe trotter. My travels included the Peoples Republic of China many times, Japan, Vietnam, Moscow, St. Petersburg, India, Nepal, Jordan, Saudi Arabia, United Arab Emirates, Kuwait, Bahrain, Argentina, Chili, Peru, Ecuador where I stood on the Equator line, Colombia, and Panama. Sometimes I spent as much as two months or more of a year in China.

I met Michael Lee, an American Chinese who wanted to contract solely with an American university to send Chinese students. I outlined what Texas universities had done with the Malaysian Ministry of Education and drew a comparison of how the University of North Alabama and his proposal could work. With the one-child policy in China, parents had saved money to send their children to the States to study. Universities were interested in hosting international students because international student tuition was higher than in-state students. We agreed.

Nga Dinh was a Vietnamese student who worked with me in the Office of International Affairs at UNA. She accompanied me to Vietnam to meet with various university officials and creditable agencies in Ho Chi Min and Hanoi. Our meeting was God's plan. Forrest and I are now godparents to Nga and Tai's daughter, Mai and son, Vu. I even experienced the delivery of Mai. I never thought I would be in a delivery room. Forrest and I have had more fun being Meme and Paopaw.

Nga, Tai, Mai, and Vu

Forrest accompanied me to Jordan, Saudi Arabia, and the UAE in 2009. We had dinner in Jeddah with Sol Bou-Nacklie who was the first President of the International Student Association at TCU in 1973. Sol was doing well and living in a 20,000 square foot villa. Many meetings were scheduled with agencies in Jeddah on the Red Sea and in Riyadh. I had to wear a loose fitting, long length cloak called abaya which the Saudi female students loaned me and the head scarf which continuously fell down over my face. I had several productive meetings in Saudi Arabia and the UAE resulting in students enrolling at UNA.

While I was in recruiting sessions in Dubai, Forrest went fishing in the Arabian Gulf and caught a large barracuda and some other fish of that region. Being a fisherman, this was one of the highlights of his trip. In the evening we had a fabulous dinner of specialties of the region with one of my former 1982, TTU students and his family. I love Middle Eastern food.

Khalid Faradooni said, "Jacquie, I remember you showed us the illustration of the potted plant, how it wilted when the roots were pulled out of the soil, then transplanted to another pot with different soil and then perked up as it adjusted to its new pot. You compared the newly arriving international students to the plant. We arrived healthy and all excited; but after our first test, we were suffering culture shock and found ourselves at the bottom of the valley. It was in the depths of the valley that we had a growth spurt of survival. Either we stayed in the valley or we climbed out of the valley to reenter our host culture and survive. After the plant had adjusted to the new soil, it was healthy again. The same was true for international students who climbed out of the valley of culture shock. You told us reverse culture shock was the worst. It certainly was for me."

Forrest returned to Alabama, and I stayed to continue on to Abu Dhabi, Bahrain, and Kuwait. While I was in the American Embassy in Abu Dhabi, UAE, I heard that the Police Department had just awarded 200 scholarships to send students to American universities to study ESL, bachelor and masters' degrees in Criminal Justice. A perfect fit for UNA. I found the responsible person and gave information on the University of North Alabama. When I returned to the States, I visited the UAE Embassy in Washington, D. C. and met with the Educational Attaché regarding the possibility of some of these students coming to UNA.

We had a good group who studied hard and most made "A's" in their academic courses after completing English as a second language course. They were a fine group of men who left their families and babies to get an education. Now they are in leadership positions in their cities.

I remember one time, three of them came to the house to go canoeing on the creek. Forrest took them to the park a short distance from our home, and they were to canoe to our house and get out. Forrest tried to tell them how to keep the canoe balanced and how to paddle. They immediately tipped over, but could stand in the water and get back in the boat.

They should have been to the house in thirty minutes. We waited and waited. Forrest finally returned and told me to take plenty of big towels to the creek for they had fallen in. In trying to float the canoe to get out of the creek behind our home, they all fell out again, but held on to the canoe. We laughed and had the best time as Forrest grilled hamburgers.

Adventure in Moscow

Prior to my visit to Moscow in 2009, I contacted the Russian Embassy in Washington D.C. to say my visa was still current, but would expire prior to my date of departure from Moscow. I asked if I should renew my visa, and the counselor said it would not be a problem as long as it was current when I entered the country.

During my visit to meet with students who were coming to the hotel to meet me, a hotel official came to me early in the morning to say my visa was expired that I must leave now. I tried to explain that the official at the Russian Embassy in Washington D.C. said I did not have to renew my visa. None of that mattered. In essence I was a fugitive in the hotel and the officials wanted me out now.

My airplane ticket was for the next day. I had visited the American Embassy in Moscow the day before to meet with some Russian students who were interested in studying in the States. Therefore, I called to present my problem and was told in no uncertain terms, "Jacquie, get out and get out now. If you do not, you will be detained for twenty-one days in detention."

I stayed and worked until that afternoon about 4:00, but one of the hotel officials stood next to me to be sure I did not become a fugitive. The hotel officials did everything they could to get me out. They changed my airplane ticket to leave right away, and paid about $60 for an airport limousine and escorted me to the limousine. Fortunately, British Airway was my first carrier; and the clerk at the desk asked me to give her $25, my passport, and she would go to get me a one day visa so I would not be detained and would be able to visit Russia again. I got out that evening with no more problems.

I visited schools in Panama City and then had lunch by the Canal to watch the ships pass through. My hotel overlooked the Atlantic Ocean where the ships entered through the Eastern side of the Panama Canal. The Wilson Dam in Florence is much deeper than any of the Panama Canals.

Another special flight was the thrill to fly into Katmandu, Nepal and see the Mt. Everest, earth's highest mountain, so high above the clouds. What a magnificent view!

May 2011, my three year contract was over. It was sad to leave the students whom I had recruited to UNA. There was a special connection to them, their country, and to be able to talk about our experiences in their homeland.

Now students from TCU, UH, TTU, and UNA have graduated and become established in their careers, but they continue to email, Facebook, or call on my birthday or send me Mother's Day cards. Many have sent us family pictures of their new babies and special happenings in their lives. At Christmas, I email all of them our annual Christmas newsletter. All of this is the beauty of living in God's Global Village. These students have woven their places in our hearts.

I am humbled to think about the influence my actions and words may have had on so many students and their families around the world. God used me as His instrument to serve international students. I have been truly blessed as these students have touched my life.

Reflection Questions

1. How often do you have "pity parties"?
2. What kind of impact does the way you handle life's situations make on relatives, friends, and co-workers?

Action Steps

Now that you have completed this book, it is time to continue your own journey toward trusting God during the good times and bad.

Instead of having a "pity party" consider counting your blessings.

FINAL WORD

"To travel is to take a journey into yourself." (Danny Kaye)

How true are these words! As a result of the many adventures of global travel I experienced during my life's journey, I am so very different from the Jacquie I was during my humble beginnings. God empowered me to live an extraordinary life where for thirty-five years I counseled thousands of international students from over 120 different countries, and negotiated agreements in eighty countries on behalf of international students—all of which were way beyond my natural ability and strength, but I did it. God prepared me to do many tasks that surprised and challenged me.

The more I trusted God the more He empowered me to do more than I could have ever imagined sitting in that outhouse so many years ago dreaming of faraway places with strange-sounding names. There were twists, turns, and many surprises throughout my journey, but my life has been more than I could have ever dreamed or imagined.

Romans 8:28 reminds us that God is at work in all things for the good of those who love Him and are called according to His purpose. As I look back over my life, I can see how God was at work in different seasons:

1954-1955 - Surgery to remove my ovaries. *God's plan was for me to give my time to international students.*

1963-1964 - Mother's yearlong hospitalization. *I learned perseverance that I needed for the future. She gave me to God.*

1969-1971 - Fukuoka, Japan as a Journeyman. *I learned to depend more on God as He laid the foundation for my career.*

1971 - Travelling Home. *God sent angels to protect me as I journeyed home from faraway places.*

May 1973 - Daddy's Death while at TCU in Grad School; *"Tough Times Don't Last; Tough People Do" by Dr. Robert Schuler, Chrystal Cathedral really helped me.*

May 1974 - God prepared a place for me at UH to be the international counselor to government-sponsored students. *God introduced me to South Main Baptist Church and Forrest.*

2003-2015 - Forrest with health issues. *Deeper faith and trust in God.*

2008 to present - Nga Dinh and I met at UNA. *Through her, we are experiencing the love of being grandparents to her precious children.*

2011-2015 - No job. *Listened to God's call to write,* ***From the Outhouse to the World.***

God has a specific plan and journey for you as well. Take what you learned from God through my life and go enjoy your own journey. Build a relationship with God. Believe, have Faith, Trust God, and you can be greater than you could ever dream/imagine.

CPSIA information can be obtained
at www.ICGtesting.com
Printed in the USA
LVHW01s0008150718
583767LV00008B/135/P